MW00471814

INTENTIONAL
4PLAY

INTENTIONAL 4PLAY

A GUIDEBOOK TO PREPARE YOU FOR THE LOVE THAT'S ALIGNED WITH YOU

SYDNEY ALLEN, LCPC & LES ALLEN, JR.

Copyright 2022 by Sydney Allen & Les Allen, Jr.

All rights reserved. No part of this publication may be reproduced, distributed, or transmitted in any form or by any means, including photocopying, recording, or other electronic or mechanical methods, without the prior written permission of the publisher, except in the case of brief quotations embodied in critical reviews and certain other noncommercial uses permitted by copyright law. If you would like permission to use material from the book (other than for review purposes), please contact the author or publisher. Thank you for your support of the author's rights.

Books may be purchased in bulk quantity and/or special sales by contacting the publisher.

Published by Mynd Matters Publishing
715 Peachtree Street NE
Suites 100 & 200
Atlanta, GA 30308

www.myndmatterspublishing.com

978-1-957092-33-1 (pbk)
978-1-957092-34-8 (ebk)

FIRST EDITION

*"Most people don't aim too high and miss.
They aim too low and hit."*
—Bob Moawad

Contents

Part 1: Introduction: Our Stories 9

Part 2: Our Intention 19

Part 3: Our Facts, Not Feelings 21

Part 4: Our Necessary Failures 22

Part 5: Learning Intentionality 23

Part 6: Learning and Loving Yourself 25

Part 7: Determining Your Commandments 36

Part 8: Swimming in The Right Pool 44

   STEP 1: Dates 1 – 3 *"Working On Myself"* 49

      1-A: Overlapping Values 49

      1-B: You Are What You Think 54

      1-C: Trust First, Then Commitment 59

      1-D: To Listen & To Share 65

      1-E: Faith 70

      1-F: Evenly Yoked 75

      1-G: Making Our Work, Work! 80

      1-H: Screen Time 86

      1-I: Open Wounds & Guarded Hearts 93

   STEP 2: Dates 4 – 6 *"My Circle of Life"* 98

      2-A: Accountability Circle 98

      2-B: All In The Family 105

2-C: Time Won't Give Me Time..................................110

2-D: Bankrupting Relationships..........................114

2-E: Netflix or The Game 118

2-F: Beyond Superficial 122

STEP 3: Dates 7 – 9 *"My Future"*.........................126

3-A: Date Night...126

3-B: Envisioning Tomorrow 130

3-C: In Sickness and In Health 134

STEP 4: Dates 10 – 12 *"My Intent"*.......................139

4-A: When I Think Of Home.............................139

4-B: More Than Four Walls................................143

4-C: Life is What You Bake It! 147

4-D: Furry Family Members 151

4-E: Hang All The Mistletoe..............................155

4-F: Planned Escapes...159

4-G: Becoming One...163

4-H: Saving The Best For Last 168

Part 9: Our Intentional Love Loving Intentionally.....................174

Our Thanks...177

Special Acknowledgments..179

Part 1

Introduction: Our Stories

"I'm a movement by myself but I'm a force when we're together. I'm good all by myself, but baby you, you make me better. As FA-BU-LO-US said in his 2011 hit, "you plus me, it equals BETTER MATH."
—Fabolous ft. Ne-Yo, Make Me Better (2011)

Sydney's Story

Alignment: a position of agreement or alliance.

Before Les and I met, we both endured a number of relationships in which we were not aligned. Although there are some experiences we don't regret, the ones we do taught us valuable lessons indeed. Of all the lessons learned, the one that permeates the depth of our souls is the importance—the NECESSITY—of identifying early whether or not you are in alignment with a potential partner. If the answer is no, despite any other emotional space you are in, you must MOVE ON. When we skipped this step, we not only squandered time, we wasted our energy, were robbed of our peace, and in some instances, our financial well-being.

Being aligned is synonymous with being in symmetry, in uniformity, with equilibrium, consistency, evenness, congruency, regularity. It is the most crucial determinant in a new partnership.

Well, it was fall of 2019 and I decided to give the dating sites one more try. One of my closest friends, who I'd encouraged to get on a dating site, found her future husband and has now been happily married for over six years. At forty-eight, I wasn't going to the club, I'd canceled my gym membership, and frequenting T.G.I.Friday's and Grace's on Thursdays after work was getting old.

My previous two and a half year relationship had dissolved six months prior and I wanted companionship. In hindsight, that mindset was one of my downfalls, but, I'll get back to the story.

I had spent the last six months doing me, redecorating my home, shopping, self-care activities out the wazoo, and helping my son get on track for his senior year of high school. Both my daughters were on their own, pursuing their dreams, and living their best lives. Now it was my time.

I was married to my first husband for fifteen years. From our marriage, I had my three babies. In retrospect, my ex and I weren't aligned, but I do attribute much of our misalignment to our age and inexperience. We were very young and still learning ourselves. As mentioned previously, you have to know and love yourself first to even consider aligning with a partner. However, no regrets because during those early years, I had the opportunity to stay home and raise my children, attend graduate school, pursue my master's in Counseling, become licensed as a therapist, and learn from first-hand experience about relationships—the joys and the pains.

So having been single for quite some time, I was ready (another mental pitfall) for a committed relationship. I met him in the fall. He was newly separated but not yet divorced. I had been divorced for nine years. In the early stages, our talk was aligned, but I quickly realized our actions were not. This led to confusion, frustration, and me feeling constantly perplexed.

When I questioned the plans for moving forward, where ultimately we were headed, I was met with a blank stare and was told, "Let's just live for today." Now understand that this man was a planner in every aspect of his life. That was part of my initial attraction. His finances were in order, his schedule to pick up his son was planned through the year's end, and his daily work and evenings were structured with minimal deviation. Yet, in terms of us, it was left to haphazard happenstance and I was essentially asked not to press the subject. When I pressed it, his response was, "You just are never happy, never satisfied."

No, we were not ALIGNED and I knew it early, yet I continued. We weren't aligned but I had become emotionally attached. We weren't aligned and I ignored the obvious. I continued to date this man, just date, without even an introduction to the most significant people in his life. When I questioned it, as we were close to the one-year mark, he stated, "It's not time and you need to trust me on this one." Funny that there didn't seem to be a timeline on other activities. I'm just saying. Misaligned.

On Labor Day 2020, I attended my cousin's wedding. When the wedding concluded, I knew in my mind that my relationship had concluded too! Witnessing their exchange of vows was life-changing for me. Seeing, feeling, and experiencing the energy from two people who were aligned and placing each other first—

before GOD, family, and friends without hesitation, confusion, trickery, or delay, was all I needed. I decided from that moment on, my journey in love would be intentional. Our trajectories had to align and that was the only way.

I sent a text and ended the relationship. I felt empowered. I'm sure there was a conversation after but it was irrelevant.

The best and the most significant growth was the metamorphosis that occurred in me during that time. There was a spiritual awakening as I had to learn to trust and lean on God and not to my own understanding—as my momma used to say. So, I prepared myself for love, intentional love, and started working in my journal. Little did I know that it would pave the way for this guidebook today.

I would never ever be accused of creating stress or drama by being intentional about my desires. No more gaslighting! Never! Nevah!

Les' Story

I've always considered myself to be an upright man. Though, in the past, I've done some very childish things. I've done my best to be an honest, dependable, and trustworthy man but I'll be the first to tell you that I have not always lived up to my goals. As any human does, we learn and grow. Even as we write this book, we are growing.

I married my first wife shortly after graduating from college. We met in my hometown of Grand Rapids, Michigan, otherwise known as "South Afrikkka North." We were introduced to one another shortly after I partied, worked out, and womanized my way out of graduate school at Michigan State University.

We were young and believed we were going to conquer the world of business. But we didn't ask enough questions to realize we had two very different ideas of how to accomplish this. She was born in Sri Lanka and raised in Nigeria. She was an intellectual that lived for colorful and loud debates–especially at home. My preference was to come home to decompress after a hard day of "puttin in work" to conquer the world.

Taught to be fiscally conservative, she sharpened that mindset by earning two undergraduate business degrees. She would then go on to obtain her MBA shortly after giving birth to our oldest daughter.

I, on the other hand, graduated with a liberal arts degree from Hampton University (Class of 1990) and received my MBA with a concentration in "Hood Rich" entrepreneurship via the Buster & Shirley Allen Academy. After earning my prestigious MBA, I didn't plan on working for anyone or any company for too long. This mindset was destined to create tension in our marriage.

She was seeking a stable middle-class life with few to no risks. And I operated in the mindset of "no risk, no reward." On top of that, she was a saver and I was a spender. She drove our 1990 Nissan Pathfinder until the wheels fell off and I was flippin' vehicles like I was Floyd Mayweather, Jr. My belief was, "I have to look the part in order to get the part!"

I started putting the final "screws" in our marriage's "coffin" when I bought an S-Class Mercedes Benz and shortly thereafter, opened a nightclub with two of my fraternity brothers. My level of maturity wasn't where it needed to be to operate this type of business without creating personal issues. This and other challenges led to our divorce. The best and most important part of this story is that our daughters have grown up and are doing very well for themselves. And she and I have matured, recognized our parts in our failed marriage, and have repaired our friendship.

Smokin' Out the Window

My second marriage can also be called "Da 180 Degree Rotation." When I look back on why I was attracted to my second wife, I believe she was a 180-degree shift from my first wife. They were complete opposites! I liked her style and it caused me to relax a few of my non-negotiables (definitely a bad idea) just to be with her.

We had a busy marriage, blending children, relocating to Texas, and starting a new business. Things appeared to be solid as we launched our mission, at least that's what I thought, until our satellite (marriage), fell back to earth. But that's what happens when you try to build a spaceship with auto parts.

The summer of 2015 was an incredibly difficult and trying time—for me personally and for my second marriage. When I learned about what was going on right up under my nose, it caused me to question my belief in the institution of marriage. I chose to stay and did what I thought would make that marriage work, and me happy.

By Fall of that year, I was exhibiting all of the characteristics of a happy, self-confident, and successful businessman. My bank account was looking strong, I was in pretty good shape, and I was able to be selective with the type of projects I chose to take on.

But I was also very empty on the inside. My marriage was held together by a shoestring, and I wanted to feel better. One weekend, while hanging out with my brother-in-law in Houston, I saw her and my breath was instantly taken away. I was totally enamored by her, and I had to have her so I quickly and confidently approached her. Within a few days, she was mine.

Shortly thereafter, I called one of my college buddies that lived in Houston and told him I was in town and wanted to meet with him one evening. Being a connoisseur of the finer things in life, he chose a well-lit, well-known bar near downtown for us to meet. The evening we met, I drove slowly past the bar, with my windows down and sunroof open. Yeah, I was "fish bowlin" and when my classmate saw me, his face lit up with a devilishly proud smile. Here I was, a confident looking Black man approaching a classy urban establishment with this "stunna." That was an interesting night.

Being inside of her made me feel EMPOWERED. She was beautiful and gave the impression that I was a successful and powerful Black man. But because I wasn't whole, I still felt empty. Having her in my life only put a bandage on my emptiness. But hell, who wouldn't think that owning a banging 2013 Porsche Panamera wouldn't help alleviate some of my depression and some of the negative thoughts I had about myself. I knew when I purchased her that she wouldn't fill the void for long. But it was worth trying. Right?

I was burning through expensive front tires on her and I took her to my mechanic for an alignment. About an hour after he began the service, he came out and asked me to come into the service area with him. He told me they had tried everything they could to get the car into alignment, but it just would not get there. They were confused, so they began to perform a forensic inspection of the suspension and frame. They soon discovered that her frame had been damaged. It had been straightened and welded back together. But the accident and subsequent repair left the frame slightly shorter on one side, thus making the car permanently out of alignment.

I did the only thing I could do without trying to purchase a new front tire every four months, I sold her. "Porscha" was permanently out of my life.

Just like my car was out of alignment and beyond repair, so was I, personally and spiritually. Around that same time, I went back to church and Bible study regularly and became more in alignment with God. But as I soon discovered, being aligned with God and following His directives are two different things entirely.

God spoke clearly to me one night while I was praying. He responded to my prayers with a directive, but I didn't act on it immediately. I know that because of my inaction/disobedience, I lost precious time, money, and I missed the window of opportunity that God had opened for me. Perhaps He had created an opening for me so I didn't have to fall so far and hard, and even cushioned my fall so I didn't have to start over on my knuckles. This happened as a result of me not immediately obeying God's direction. Instead, I questioned what I clearly heard Him say. And, as a result, I had to lose everything, including myself (I snoozed, so I had to lose). In hindsight, losing everything prepared me for my rehabilitation and realignment and my readiness for the future that was planned for me.

I share this because somehow it was a wake-up call for me. I realized that yes, I was looking damn good on the outside, had a nice bank account and a brand-new house. But I didn't feel good at all, as though something was eating me from the inside out. That feeling affected me no matter how much I worked out or how good I thought I looked in a suit. I just wasn't right. I realized that I had to be realigned not only with myself, but also with God. I had to permanently remove the infection that was destroying me in order to begin my healing process. It started with filing for divorce.

In January 2017, I walked away from a brand new, fully furnished, 3,400 square foot marital house (yes house, we all know that a house is not a home) to begin the process of rebuilding myself. I rented a one-bedroom apartment in The Colony, a city north of Dallas. I didn't have any furniture or any pots or pans. All I had were my clothes, my pickup truck, and my "Sunday" vehicle. I slept on an inflatable mattress that I purchased at Sam's Club, and it provided me with the best sleep of my life. I was at peace.

One of the awesome side effects of my terrible situation was that I had become a gym rat and I was in the best shape of my life. This made meeting new women and dating easy.

DATING DURING AND AFTER D2
Return of Da Jedi | Sky Walking

The intensity of the crash and burn ending of my second marriage took its toll on me mentally, physically, and emotionally. Between

July 2015 and January 2017, I had lost who I was as a person. I lost belief in myself, I lost my swag, and I was dead ass broke.

The best and most important growth that occurred within me during that time, was the strengthening of my relationship with God. I had moved towards being in much better alignment with Him. I know that growing my personal relationship with God is the only reason I am still walking this earth. There is no way that I shouldn't be dead, locked up, or smelling like smoke after walking away from that intentionally lit grease fire of a marriage. Let me clarify, the entire marriage wasn't bad. The first seven years were good. But those last few years were LIT and not in a good way.

Not only was I starting over financially, I was also starting over mentally. The last few years of that marriage were a severe haze. I was broken all the way down to my brake pads! It was like I was pledging again but I didn't have an organized support system to rebuild me. I felt like I wasn't worthy of having a decent life, nor a decent wife/partner. I was beat down. And because I was too ashamed to talk about my condition with my core support group, I began the journey of my rehabilitation in solitude.

Little did I know, the difficult road I traveled and my harsh rehabilitation would ultimately prepare me for creating this guidebook as a tool to spare others from brokenness, financial ruin, and loss of self.

Part 2
Our Intention

We have written this guidebook as a tool to assist you in getting to know yourself and your potential partner in an *intentional* way. Hopefully, it will equip you with important tools that will allow you to make well-informed decisions prior to becoming seriously involved with someone.

Most of us do our homework, or due diligence, before we make an important business decision and/or expensive purchase. But for some reason, we typically don't do the same for our love lives. Why wouldn't we do the same before we make a partnership decision? A life partner/dating decision could alter the trajectory of one's life forever. Just think about it, if you don't choose the right person, these are just a few of the many consequences that can result:

- *Single parenthood*
- *Financially damaged*
- *Emotionally scarred*
- *Physically damaged*
- *...Or Worse*

In our society, we tend to allow physical attraction, which we all know fades over time, to drive most of our relationship decisions. Why not use direct feedback from questions in this book to assist with determining compatibility? Spend some focused time to better determine these odds before you share your time and your body with someone.

The more you learn about your potential partner early on, the better. You should get to know each other:

- Spiritually
- Emotionally
- Intellectually
- And then, Physically

Sydney and I have read in multiple publications, and have learned this from our own personal experiences, that marriages based primarily on emotion end in divorce almost 50% of the time. Arranged or less emotionally-based marriages, however, have a greater chance of sustainability. Couples in the latter scenarios only file for divorce between 4% and 8% of the time. Emotions shouldn't be the primary driver of your decision to marry as there are many other factors to consider.

In "Why you should treat marriage more like a business," Dr. Joseph Cilona states: *"When it comes to dating, many people use their emotions as a compass for navigating love and romance, and emotions often play the primary role in decision making and behavior. For those that want to make better decisions when it comes to dating and romance, it's important to remember that there are often many variables that influence compatibility and compliment your love and marriage, and that feelings are just a part of a much larger picture."* (Danielle Page, *Better By Today*, June 30, 2017)

Part 3
Our Facts, Not Feelings

As a business owner, I have learned to remove emotion almost entirely from any decision I need to make as it tends to cloud my ability to make the best, or the most profitable, decision. Don't get me wrong, I have personal feelings about most important matters, but I don't let feelings solely dictate or drive my decision while ignoring the facts. Shouldn't we do the same thing when we're choosing a life partner?

Using *Intentional 4Play* correctly will assist you with the facts via your research (the questions). Facts make relationships work. Feelings allow relationships to grow.

By purchasing this book, you've taken the first step to intentionally change your love life from a somewhat haphazard journey to a self-directed choice. Let's change your thoughts, from "Hopefully I will meet my bride/groom/soulmate someday" to "Today I will intentionally choose a bride/groom/soulmate with whom I am aligned."

Part 4
Our Necessary Failures

Your past is your past. The hope is that you've learned from it and are tired of repeating the same mistakes you made in the past. We're hoping you are determined to try a new method to reach your goals. Are you ready to start a new chapter in your life? One that can be your best. If so, let's get started!

It's not good enough to have good intentions to do anything. As poet Samuel Johnson is credited with saying, "Hell is paved with good intentions." Statistics say that while you may have the desire to change how you select your partner, most of you reading these pages will never start living your dating/courting life as intentionally as needed in order to choose the perfect partner. But the best part is that the choice is yours. It is up to you not to fall or fail into that category again.

We truly understand having failures in love. We had many failures in love before we finally decided that we had enough of doing the same things and expecting a different outcome. This guide is our way to help you avoid the same, or as many, errors as we did. Today is the day for you to become tired of watching other people choose their spouses/partners and living their lives fulfilled, while you're sitting on the sidelines wondering why it isn't you. Starting today, choose to live every part of your life with intention, especially your love life.

Part 5
Learning Intentionality

My parents were intentional, especially when it came to monitoring my circle of friends, even at a very early age. Growing up in the hood, they knew who they allowed in my circle would either be a help or a huge hindrance to my future success. Therefore, they made our house the neighborhood gathering place so they could meet, know, and monitor almost everyone with which I associated.

They would tell me, "That boy is Shady," or "Erik is cool," or "That girl is nasty!" They supervised my building or dismantling of relationships to increase my chances of being successful. Sometimes I didn't like the interference because my friend was the cool kid, but they knew he didn't have the same or similar upbringing that I did so hanging with him may potentially take me off the track they had planned for me. My parents track/plan was simply college, or college, or college.

My parents were very intentional about who they would allow in my life. You have to be just as intentional or more intentional with everything you want to achieve, especially your love life. If the sexy or handsome person you like (or believe you want to be with), doesn't meet your minimum standards for partnership—your non-negotiables—they have to be put in either the acquaintance zone or left completely alone. If not, they will take you off your success track, one way or another.

As author John Maxwell says, wishing, hoping, dreaming and

visualizing is not enough. "Only by managing my thinking and shifting my thoughts from desire to deeds would I be able to bring about positive change. I needed to go from wanting to doing." He also says, "An unintentional life accepts everything and does nothing. An intentional life embraces only the things that will add to the mission of significance."

Part 6
Learning and Loving Yourself

Before you set your sights on being the perfect partner for your perfect partner, take some quality time to discover the authentic you. Then take time to love the person you discover you are.

Once you take this time to rediscover you and what really makes you happy, sad, angry, and most importantly, at peace, you will not allow yourself to settle for anyone other than someone that meets all of your specific criteria. Your love of self will outweigh anyone's looks, money, and status. If the person that you are with, or want to be with, meets some of your criteria but not all of it, in a matter of time, you will pay a heavy price to be with that person.

This criteria is called your list of non-negotiables. Your non-negotiables list is like your vision board for your future partner. People always tell us to visualize our goals." What we are saying is visualize the must-have traits of your future partner.

And don't stop there. You must then actively pursue that match. You have to realize, and remember, that you have developed and memorialized your non-negotiables for very specific reasons, ultimately for your peace and happiness. Because when you truly love yourself, you won't compromise your non-negotiables to be with anyone.

At the end of the day, your non-negotiables were developed specifically for you, for your specific needs. I suggest you treat your list of non-negotiables like they say you should treat your dream ideas. Don't share with many, just pursue them accordingly.

The questions below will help you look within and have an opportunity to have some self-analysis, self-clarification, and ease your ability to make informed decisions. You'll want to ask yourself some of these questions prior to becoming intentionally involved with someone, and others should be asked while you're with your partner and deciding whether or not you're going to intentionally court.

QUESTIONS TO ASK YOURSELF
ABOUT YOURSELF

1. Who am I? How would I describe myself?
2. Do I want a committed partner or need a committed partner?
3. What is my primary love language? My secondary love language? (*The free "5 Love Languages" quiz is available at www.5lovelanguages.com/quizzes/love-language*)
4. What did I learn about myself from my last three relationships?
5. Am I mentally over my last three relationships?
6. Am I sexually over my last relationship?
7. What strengths do I bring to a relationship?
8. What liabilities do I bring to a relationship?
9. Am I taking the best physical care of myself so I can have a healthy life with my partner?
10. What is it like to be in a relationship with me?
11. What do I love about myself the most?

12. What am I willing to work on to be the best partner I can be?

13. What am I willing to let go of to be the best partner I can be?

14. What makes me happy in a relationship?

15. What makes me sad in a relationship?

16. What makes me angry in a relationship?

17. When do I feel safe in a relationship?

18. What makes me feel unsafe in a relationship?

19. Where should I make more effort when it comes to a relationship?

20. What is the best word to describe me in a committed relationship?

Notes

_____

_____

_____

_____

_____

_____

_____

_____

TIPS FOR ASKING AND ANSWERING QUESTIONS

Asking questions is a great way to start conversations for people that are getting to know each other and/or reconnecting. With the right questions, the two of you can get to know each other on a much deeper level while still keeping things fun and light. Even if you're both answering questions one after another, this can be fun! But, this activity could go south pretty fast if one, or both of you, treat it as an interrogation.

Before you try out our list of questions, here are some tips to keep in mind, in no particular order, when asking and answering questions to help ensure you and your potential partner both have a good time.

1. Remember, honesty builds trust
Be honest with your potential partner while answering these questions.

2. Be open, don't be afraid
If you and your potential partner are meant for each other, you should be able to talk about everything. So don't be afraid of talking about deep topics like a low credit score, a health issue, or a drama-filled ex.

3. Don't rush each other
Some questions may make your potential partner feel uncomfortable. Avoid rushing each other into answering everything. Stay patient, some things take time.

4. Don't be judgmental

You may not understand every thought of your partner, that's normal. Keep an open mind because we all have different backgrounds and experiences.

Questions to ask each other that are thought provoking, fun, and could make for some interesting conversation.

- What part of yourself are you holding back currently?
- Where in your life are you making unhelpful assumptions?
- On your deathbed, what do you think you'll regret doing/ not doing as you think back over your life?
- What seemingly insignificant thing contributes greatly to your happiness?
- If you could only hold on to five physical items, what would you keep and why?
- What part of your life have you still not figured out?
- If people came with a warning label, what would yours say?
- What's a very ordinary action you find really attractive?
- What is something you want to ask me but are afraid to ask?
- Name three things we have in common.
- How do you best receive criticism?
- Who deserves credit in your life that you've been slow to acknowledge?
- If someone wanted to annoy you easily, what would they have to do?
- What moment do you wish you could relive and even change?

- What piece of advice would you give your younger self and why?
- How are you able to love someone that you don't agree with?
- What do you do better than anyone else you know?
- How do you let yourself down?
- When was the last time you took a leap of faith and found out you can fly?
- What do you want to know about your potential partner that you have been afraid to ask?
- What big decision in your life felt scary at the time, but looking back was the best decision you could have made?
- What part of the problem are you not accepting that you may be an active participant to?
- What do you worry that you will never get over?
- Where are you settling where you could be thriving?
- What's the skeleton in your closet?
- What choice had the greatest impact on your life?
- What makes you a good partner?
- What are you most fearful of?
- What's something you try to actively avoid in life?
- If you could travel back in time for one day, what year would it be and why?
- Have you ever broken someone's heart? Has your heart been broken?
- Are you an optimist, pessimist, or realist?
- Do you prefer to love or be loved?

- What's your go-to funny story?
- What are you looking forward to that's happening soon?
- How much social interaction is too much?
- What small things brighten up your day when they happen?
- What do you care least about?
- What are people often surprised to learn about you?
- What says the most about a person?
- Who is the most fascinating person you've met?
- What are your favorite alcoholic and non-alcoholic drinks?
- What are you kind of obsessed with these days?
- What are some things you believe everyone should try at least once?
- If you were given one year to live, what would you change about how you spend your time?
- Describe your perfect day.
- Tell me about someone you no longer speak to that you wish you were still friends with.
- Tell me about the most recent kind thing you did for a stranger.
- What's something you're really good at?
- What's your favorite thing to do by yourself?
- What is the greatest accomplishment of your life thus far?
- What do you consider to be the biggest mistake you've ever made?
- Tell me about a time you felt completely out of your comfort zone.
- What's the biggest risk you've ever taken? Would you do it again?

- Would you rather be very famous or very wealthy?
- In what circumstances, if any, is it okay to lie?
- What do you worry about the most?
- What do you wish more people recognized you for?
- What's something you wish you were better at?
- Name something that's always worth splurging on.
- Would you rather travel the world or have the house of your dreams?
- What motivates you professionally?
- When is the last time you put a lot of effort into something outside of work or school?
- What are you looking forward to that's happening soon?
- How much social interaction is too much?
- What small things brighten up your day when they happen?
- What is your predominant love language?
- Tell me about your first heartbreak.
- When was the first time you said "I love you" to someone who isn't a member of your family?
- What's a very ordinary action that you find really attractive?
- What is your favorite memory of us?
- Describe the physical touch that best communicates "I love you."
- Tell me about someone you no longer speak to that you wish you were still friends with.
- Tell me about the most recent kind thing you did for a stranger.
- What's something you're really good at?

- What's your favorite thing to do by yourself?
- What do you consider to be the biggest mistake you've ever made?
- Tell me about a time you felt completely out of your comfort zone.
- What's the biggest risk you've ever taken? Would you do it again?
- Would you rather be very famous or very wealthy?
- What do you worry about the most?
- What's something you wish you were better at?
- If you could stay stuck in one decade, what decade would it be?
- If you could be reincarnated, who would you come back as?

Notes

_____

_____

_____

_____

_____

_____

_____

_____

Part 7
Determining Your Commandments:
Your Non-Negotiables

You may be wondering what is the best way to determine your non-negotiables. We believe it should be based on your value system and the promises you want to keep to yourself, your family, and your potential partner. Below is a list of examples of non-negotiables.

Examples of Non-Negotiables:
- Being of Good Character
- Attractiveness
- Being Educated
- Non-Smoker
- Non-Drinker or a Social Drinker
- Family Oriented
- Churchgoer
- Living a Healthy Lifestyle
- Gainfully Employed
- No Children or No Children at Home
- Preference of Geographical Location
- Current Marital Status (Never Married/Divorced)
- Similar Interests

Your list may be similar to these examples or be very different. Regardless, there is no negotiating your non-negotiables. They are your chosen principles and you should not compromise. They embody what you will and won't accept from others. This list is yours, own it. Do not be apologetic about it. These rules are your compass for your journey. If you steer away, you will become lost and perhaps be the ride or die that just died!

TYPICAL REASONS WE IGNORE OR COMPROMISE OUR NON-NEGOTIABLES

- Attractiveness
- Convenience
- Fear
- Damaged from Past Hurt(s)
- Low Self-Esteem
- Financial Situation
- Wealth of Potential Partner
- Fear of Being Alone
- Fitting In
- Settling
- Age
- Pressure from Friends, Family or Children
- Loneliness

In those relationships where I neglected to have specified non-negotiables, or didn't stick to it, I faced challenges that had more to do with my choice than the problem itself. For example, if I am a disciplined saver, and I choose a reckless spender, shopping to post selfies on the "gram," there will be frustration. In this case,

I cannot be frustrated with their spending, which was revealed early on, but rather my continued pursuit of this person despite knowing this incompatibility.

As relationships are reflective, you want to ensure the same qualities you are looking for, you can offer. Studies show that although opposites attract, people with similar attributes have a higher yield of relationship success. In choosing a mate by seeking out those things that are important to you, you can enhance your chance of a more balanced and harmonious partnership.

Questions To Ask Yourself About Your Potential Partner

1. Do they meet ALL of your checklist items? If not, why are you considering this person as a partner?

2. Do they meet ALL of your checklist items? If not, why are you considering this person as a partner?

3. Do they meet ALL of your checklist items? If not, why are you considering this person as a partner?

4. Do they meet ALL of your checklist items? If not, why are you considering this person as a partner?

5. Do they meet ALL of your checklist items? If not, why are you considering this person as a partner?

This may sound more difficult than it is but you must start by getting in the right pool. If you're looking for ocean perch you're not going fishing in Lake Michigan. Similarly, if you're looking for YSL, you should not be at Target.

Let me clarify, you can compromise once you have met someone that's aligned with you. Compromise is a needed component in any successful relationship. There's just no compromise in your selection process. When looking for a particular ingredient for a cake, there are some things that can't be substituted otherwise the cake won't rise, or stick together, or even taste good. Save yourself time from having to bake another cake. You've experimented enough, right? Right?! Perfect your recipe. It's less difficult when you're determined to master it and not let it master you!

LES' NON-NEGOTIABLES

I learned that meeting successful women with great character and integrity would not be an issue for me. Since my divorce, I've dated ambitious women with successful careers. But without fail, each of these relationships would end. Most didn't end because of something they had necessarily done or not done, as I would soon learn. Through counseling, and my awareness of my non-negotiables, the relationships ended because of me. I carried too much baggage and had not taken the proper time to learn myself and stand steadfast to my non-negotiables.

After this realization, I made a point of sticking to my checklist of characteristics and "things" that I desired my future partner to embody and to believe. To some, my checklist was shallow, but I developed it around what I believed, and still believe, would bring me to my ultimate long-term peace and happiness. When putting my checklist together, I went back in time to think about when and where I was happiest. And what made me believe and feel that I was happy. I didn't want to spend the last days of my life being anything but content. I knew one cannot be happy all the time. But when given the opportunity to select a partner who will give me/us the best chance of living out our lives, why shouldn't I be selective and dream big?

My future wife must be and/or possess these:

- Godly (fearing and loving)
- Honest, Transparent & Loyal
- Have no children younger than 18
- A college graduate (preferably from an HBCU; preferably a private HBCU; preferably Hampton)
- A member of a "Divine Nine" Sorority (sorry, not sorry)
- Employed (full-time)
- Have a Healthy Lifestyle
- Beautiful (inside and out)

Each of the items on my non-negotiable list have a very significant backstory attached to them (perhaps I'll share in a future book). I didn't always stick to this list, which I believe resulted in the demise of several of my relationships. I had intentionally and purposefully created my non-negotiable list, therefore I needed to utilize it to have a solid chance at the life and love that I desired. Again, to some, it may seem shallow, but for me it held the key ingredients for MY building a successful and long lasting love.

LEARNING THE HARD WAY

As I stated earlier, I took some serious time after my divorce to dive within myself to rediscover who I was, what was important to me, and to become grounded in myself and my desires. After I did this, I was sharing my non-negotiables with a family member, and she let me know that I was shallow and petty, in her opinion, for creating and attempting to fall in love with someone that met this criteria.

Internally, I began to question my list and sure enough, I started making exceptions for the next three women I dated. After several months of being in those relationships, I realized it was one thing or a few things I compromised on my non-negotiable list that began to push me away. I ended up wasting our time, energy, and money. The worst part is that people's feelings were hurt. The moral of the story—stick to your non-negotiables.

SYDNEY'S NON-NEGOTIABLES

Non-negotiables? What non-negotiables? Because I didn't take the time to love myself and set standards not to be compromised, I can honestly say I had none. One might say I had an imaginary list I referenced but zero adherence. In other words, I spoke of certain criteria yet accepted characteristics and qualities I should not have and justified them each and every time. I settled and thought I could fix, mold, or somehow work my magic with my mate. The truth is, sadly, I was in denial from the start and with every red flag waving boldly, I still chose to proceed.

To make matters worse, each time a relationship ended, I

didn't allow myself ample time to process what went wrong, or even correlate how my choice could have contributed to the relationship's ultimate demise. One of my BFF's used to always say, you have to get comfortable being alone. This act alone could have saved me valuable time and unnecessary heartache.

After my aha moment, I decided I had to change this predestined doomed course. I put myself first and thought about the qualities I needed in a mate to move forward, those I possessed, and the qualities my potential mate had to possess to greatly increase the probability of alignment. After all, why shouldn't I be selective and dream big?

My future husband must be and/or possess these:
- Spiritual
- Honest and Transparent
- Attractive
- Kind
- Good Communicator
- College Graduate
- Gainfully Employed/Financially Stable
- Good Decision Maker
- Flexible
- Family Oriented
- Supportive

Many times in dating, I went off of my "vibes," and what I like to call chemistry. I had to learn the hard way that chemistry and compatibility were completely different. Chemistry may get you in the door but compatibility keeps you in the house.

Notes

Part 8
Swimming in The Right Pool

You can't put any type of fish in any body of water and get the best results. Remember when you brought a new fish home from the pet store? You couldn't put it into an existing fish tank without completing a few crucial steps. One was allowing it to sit in its own bag of water so it would get acclimated to the temperature of its new tank. And actually, this was the last step of the laundry list of steps you had to take to successfully introduce your new fish into its new environment.

But prior to that, in order to guarantee survival, there was a process. First, you had to go to the pet store. Then, you had to determine the type of aquatic life you could add to your aquarium. Did you have a freshwater or saltwater tank? Did you have a five gallon, twenty-five gallon, or fifty-five gallon tank? Were your existing fish tropical or not? Could they be maintained in all water temperatures? Then, once you confirmed these items, you had to go to the right section/aisle and choose the appropriate fish, invertebrates, snakes, lizards, frogs, or amphibians, etc. that could not only survive but thrive in your aquarium environment.

You also had to consider what types of fish, and other creatures, could live together harmoniously. If you skipped the research, you would have missing fish, dead fish, or half-eaten fish floating in the tank daily. If you have to make this many informed decisions and take this many intentional actions prior to bringing a fish home, shouldn't you at least put twenty times more effort into preparing and bringing a new person into your life/home?

Often we loosen our non-negotiables because we have been in the same dating pool (environment) for so long that we begin merging things that don't belong together. This leads to our having uneven, broken, half-eaten, and even dead relationships. Sound familiar? Or, we may think we have exhausted all viable options in our area. There's just no one here for me who meets my requirements, maybe I'm too picky. The thought that there's "no one here" may or may not be the case. But maybe, you're just swimming aka living in the wrong body of water.

When we say you may be swimming in the wrong body of water, it may be geographical, but most times it has to do with like-mindedness. Most of us have been guilty of not being intentional enough to interact with people that had similar values, interests, and beliefs as we do while we were available/dating. We are advising you to perform the necessary due diligence and find other folks with things in common with yourself.

Here's a few ideas on how to find like-minded people:

1. **Improve your conversational skills**: Practice your conversation skills so you get to know people on a deeper level and this can create chemistry.

2. **Look for places where people share your interests & meet regularly:** You can improve your chances by going to places where people share your interests and intentionality.
   - Look for ways to meet people at recurring functions

- Go to Meetup.com and see what interests you
- Join local interest-based groups on Facebook
- Attend and/or join extracurricular activities like a Pan-Hellenic Council Meeting or activity
- Join physical meetups (e.g., 5k run, bowling league, etc.)
- Use your mutual interests and/or past experiences to start a conversation

3. **Follow-up with people that you've met in the past (or even went to school/college with):** Reach out to people you've met and know. Use your mutual experience/interest as the reason for reconnecting.

Earlier, you went through an exercise to create and memorialize (write down) your non-negotiables. These traits are important for your love, peace, and happiness. So if you have to change a few things, like your choice, your environment, and your mindset, it's the least you can do. Remember, there are plenty of fish in the sea but it takes the right bait to catch the right one.

Questions:

Are you in the right pool? (like-mindedness)

Are you the right bait? (the best version of you)

Are they the right catch? (aligned with your non-negotiables)

If no, release them and keep fishing. If yes, they're a keeper.

JUDGMENT DAY
AND YOUR VERDICT IS...

Love is Blind is a popular expression, but it doesn't have to be. Put the work in first, so you can clearly see and make a wise decision.

We make finding the right partner more complex than it has to be. If you follow this guide early on, you can determine whether or not there is enough in common with a potential partner to move forward or not. This decision is one of the most important decisions you will make as its outcome may have significant, impactful, and long term implications.

How many times have you ignored the questions or been too afraid to ask them because you didn't want to know the true answer? How many times have you continued to pursue someone that didn't have the qualities that were important to you? You were likely doing this to force an outcome you desired but knew was not sustainable. Many of us turn a blind eye to the truth to maintain an incompatible situation. This is an example of throwing your non-negotiable list straight out the window and freestyling with your life.

Throughout the course of a lifetime, there are many important investments that one makes. During most of these investments, like buying a house or a car, we are cautious, careful and deliberate in our decision making. This single investment—your potential partner—has the ability to significantly impact your children, your family, your financial position, and most importantly, your peace. Therefore, do your due diligence and choose wisely.

Pay attention to your intuition as it will provide you with the cautionary yellow flags and those stop and run red flags. That gut feeling that is rarely wrong. Acknowledge them and follow them because these are flags, not lights. Unlike traffic lights, yellow and red don't eventually turn into green.

STEP 1: Dates 1 – 3
"Working On Myself"

1-A: Overlapping Values

What rules do you live by? If you asked your potential partner that question and they replied, "Don't get caught," what would you think? And more importantly, what would you do?

When I was in my late teens, I remember thinking to myself, why do so many young ladies get involved with and have children by dealers? Many of my partners growing up were street pharmaceutical salesmen. And even they knew that 99% of them wouldn't be able to make a living, much less sustain a family doing what they were doing. Moreover, all of them understood the game well enough to know they really only had two exit opportunities once they started selling or slinging and we all knew what they were.

So, I couldn't understand why young ladies chose this route to start their journey at a known disadvantage to their peers. Many were exposed to good morals and values. Hell, I went to church with fifty percent of them! Let me reiterate, we are not supporting a settling mindset. It's okay to pursue what looks good and feels good, just make sure that Mister or Miss "Looks Good/Feels Good" also has a similar value system with goals and beliefs that align with yours.

Some of the young women hoped for the best, knowing the reality. Others chose to ignore the truth altogether.

One of the best predictors for future behavior is history. Avoid repeating the patterns that lead down the road to misery. Stop and discontinue this vicious cycle. STOP. It may not be the easiest decision, but it has proven to produce a better outcome.

I wish I had a guidebook in my late teens and even in my adulthood to assist me in navigating my choices. It sure would have saved heartache, heartbreak, and regret. Some mistakes make you better, stronger, wiser and teach you valuable lessons. Other mistakes help you grow and evolve.

Learning from mistakes is crucial. Not learning from them can lead to continual self-destruction. Strive for continual improvement when preparing for a successful relationship. Stop regretting what is preventable. "Fear regret more than failure," says Taryn Rose.

Now it's ok for you and your partner not to have exact matches in terms of values, but you certainly don't want to have values that clash. Overlapping values can be key to successful and fulfilling relationships.

Ask yourself, what are my values? Do I value hard work and education? Do I require a partner that holds these same values and lives an integrous life? What are some beliefs I have that I will not compromise? What do I stand for and what should my significant other stand for?

Asking and answering these questions early is paramount. Remember you are interviewing a person for potentially the most important, impactful role in your life. A slip in judgment here could create hardships that last at least twenty-one years if not the rest of your life.

Identify your set of rules and live by them and then choose a partner that plays and lives by a similar set. As we grow older and (hopefully) wiser, we have less time to repeatedly make the same mistakes. You've likely heard, a repeated mistake is a decision. Decide early to choose wisely.

QUESTIONS TO ASK EACH OTHER

- What does the word "value" mean to you?
- What's your North Star/guiding principle?
- Do you believe in a higher power?
- What do you value in life?
- What three words do you think others most commonly use to describe you?
- What are values that you learned early on but don't agree with now?
- What widely accepted belief needs to be dead and buried?
- What belief keeps getting you into trouble?
- What beliefs do you want to pass onto your children and grandchildren?
- If you could only teach one thing to your (future) child, what would it be?
- What do you think makes someone a good person?
- Which of your personality traits are you most proud of?
- How do you show kindness to others?
- What life lessons have you had to learn the hard way?
- Do you live by any piece of advice or motto?
- What makes you feel at peace?

- What would you refuse to give up even if you were offered 10 million dollars?
- What do you think society owes its citizens?
- Is violence ever acceptable?
- Do you believe in second chances?
- Who is the best role model a person could have?
- Who besides your parents taught you the most about life?
- If you could give everyone just one piece of advice, what would it be?
- What would you hope would be said in your eulogy?
- If you were given a year to live, what would you stop doing and what would you start?
- What is the one rule you have for yourself that you will never break?
- If you had the power to change one law, what law would you change?
- Tell me about the person you admire most that is not a celebrity.
- What are you most grateful for?
- What are you most selfish about?
- What groups do you have a negative bias towards?
- Would you party in front of your children?
- When would you lie to someone?
- How do you interact with someone who disagrees with you?
- What would you change in the world if you could?
- Are you an organ donor and how did you come to that decision?

Notes

1-B: You Are What You Think

"People that think they can and people that think they can't. Both are right."

As a child, teenager, and young adult, I struggled with what I saw as not being good enough. I remember one of my teachers telling my mom I blended in with the woodwork. Basically, I hid. I didn't talk unless I had to and didn't move around too much unless it was time to move. I followed directions, stayed in my seat, and talked when I was spoken to so that I could, in essence, go unnoticed. I did this until college when I finally came out of my shell. For too long, feelings of inadequacy impacted what I did and how I did it. My strengths, skills, and talents couldn't be actualized until I acknowledged them. Until I recognized them. Until I believed in ME.

Self-esteem refers to a person's belief about their own worth and value. It is the respect you have for yourself and your abilities. It's your confidence and your overall sense of self-worth. More importantly, it is crucial to how you function every day. When your self-esteem is "high," you feel good about yourself and feel deserving of the respect of others. When it's "low," you put little value on YOU—your output, your opinions, your ideas. Self-esteem greatly influences your life, your choices, and the relationships with those close to you.

Looking back, I heard from my mom daily how pretty and smart I was. She praised me every opportunity she could, and that's still true. Outside of our home I didn't get a whole lot of positive feedback because I didn't do anything to stand out, which was on purpose. So, all those messages I could have received to help with my self-esteem, my feelings of positive self-worth, didn't happen. The messages I did receive were from my peers and they were cruel. Unfortunately, yet predictably, their messages were the ones that stuck. Taunts like "buck tooth" and "Miss Piggy." Their words kept me from raising my hand, volunteering to stand in front of the class, and run for any office.

Some of these feelings stayed with me throughout high school and early on in college, until things turned around. My grades were looking good, I was active in some clubs and was enjoying my experience at Hampton. I fell in love with the AKAs on campus and after getting to know them and attending several interest activities, I was selected to pledge to become a member of Alpha Kappa Alpha Sorority. I was a part of a special sisterhood and my confidence grew even more.

As a psychology major, I learned quickly about esteem and how my experiences had shaped some of the inaccurate and maladaptive thought patterns I had and my feelings about myself. Not only was I in college learning about the psyche, I was actively applying that to my life, my future goals, and the desire for a healthy esteem. One's own thoughts have perhaps the biggest impact on one's esteem. You are what you think so be careful of your thoughts.

Healthy self-esteem in any relationship is so important because you can't expect someone to love you if you don't love yourself. This was a lesson I had to learn. My journey of SELF LOVE empowered me, impacted my choices and what I ultimately said "YES" or "NO" to.

Everything changes when you love yourself. You can begin to grow into who you are and let go of the person you are not. Higher self-esteem paves the way for healthier relationships and gives you the confidence so even during the toughest of times in dating or in relationships, you are strong and capable.

QUESTIONS TO ASK EACH OTHER

- What does healthy self-esteem mean to you?
- What do you love the most about you?
- When do you feel most like yourself?
- What are your three favorite qualities about yourself?
- What do you do well?
- What compliments do you struggle to believe?
- When do you feel most out of place?
- How can you help yourself improve the things that make you feel uneasy?
- What wrong assumptions do people make about you?
- Do you know anyone that has the type of confidence you hope to have?
- Describe a time when you were your own worst enemy?
- What negative messages do you constantly tell yourself?
- What would you like to know more about, but haven't had the time to look into?
- What have you done from a place of insecurity that has had long-lasting effects?

- What's the most recent thing you've done for the first time?
- How can you make yourself proud today?
- When do you feel most vulnerable?
- What do you love about yourself that you worry others will struggle to accept?
- Do you believe you are someone deserving of love?
- Do you believe you deserve happiness?
- When do you feel most protected and taken care of?
- Have you ever felt like a complete and utter failure?
- What's the one quality you wish you had but don't?
- If you were to frame and hang a quote on the wall you look at most, what would it say?
- How well do you handle criticism?

Notes

_____

_____

_____

_____

_____

_____

_____

_____

1-C: Trust First, Then Commitment

Trust is defined as the firm belief in the reliability, trust, ability or strength of someone.

Sabrina Romanoff says "Trust is the foundational component to relationships because it allows you to be vulnerable and open up to the person without having to defensively protect yourself." We agree with her because without a superior level of trust in your partner, you will never have the strong and peaceful relationship you desire.

How does your partner obtain your trust? Some say trust is earned, and for example, believe everyone you meet starts with "0" trust points. Others start people out with a certain level of trust, and allow them to gain or lose it. I tend to do the latter. Everyone I meet starts with 70 (out of 100) trust points. It's akin to starting out with a "C" (70 points) in my "trust class," which represents an average level of trust. During the course of our interactions, they either gain or lose points. As it is in other areas of life, it's always easier to lose points than it is to gain them. Now that I am older, once you get below that starting point of 70 trust points, I am moving on. And in a romantic situation, it's difficult for me to continue if you haven't built up at least 91 trust points. But that's just me.

Prior to committing to someone, you should be able to trust them 95% of the time. When being intentional, trust is an absolute key to choosing the correct partner. If you have any doubts about anything, take the time to discuss those areas before you move to the next level.

Commitment is defined as the quality of being dedicated to a cause, activity, etc.

Syd and I recommend that before you have your third contact/date with your potential partner, discuss and mutually come to an agreement of what the definition of commitment is to each of you and what it is to your relationship.

I am willing to bet that if you have purchased and are reading this book, you are ready to be with someone that wants the same level of commitment you do.

We have developed **The Allen Commitment Scale** or simplified, the ACS. The ACS is simply a 4-point scale that identifies a person's level of commitment based upon where they tell you they are.

<u>Where do you land on the ACS?</u>

Level 1: Committed to self – *Dating*

Level 2: Committed to multiple friends – *Kicking It*

Level 3: Committed to one (monogamous relationship) –
My Lady/My Man

Level 4: Fully Committed (ready for marriage) – *Wifey/
Husband (with papers/receipts)*

Many men are honest when you initially ask them what they are looking for in a relationship. When you ask a guy if he is looking for a monogamous relationship and he says "not right now, I am just dating," he's telling the truth. LISTEN TO HIM! On our scale, he is at a commitment level "1." Don't try to bend him closer to where you are.

If you are not on the same commitment level, thank him for his time and walk away. If you don't walk away, do not become upset or resentful down the road when he does something that a commitment level 1 person would do. After all, he told you where he was but you chose not to listen.

Take the time to know where you are on the scale and why. Have deep and sometimes rough discussions with your potential partner no later than your third date/contact. Use the responses you receive to make the best decision for you. The more information you know, the better choice you can make. People that are ready to be intentional in their love lives, do not waste time with people who are not at the same ACS level.

Cheating

Another topic that should be discussed no later than your third date/contact is cheating. Today, there are multiple definitions and levels of cheating. What is cheating to you? What does your potential partner consider cheating? Do you consider any of the items below cheating?

- Exchanging contact information with others
- Texting/Emailing/Calling others
- Non work-related meetings with others
- Touching others
- Sexual Intimacy with others

Discuss your answers. Take time to discuss each other's responses. Mutually establish what is acceptable and what is inappropriate in your relationship prior to committing.

QUESTIONS TO ASK EACH OTHER

- What does trust mean to you?
- What is something your potential partner could do to make you trust them even more?
- In general, how do people earn your trust?
- How does someone lose your trust?
- Would you rather someone be honest and hurt your feelings or lie and protect them?
- What areas do you think you and your potential partner would need to work on to build trust?
- Have any of your previous relationships ended due to trust issues?
- How important is honesty in a relationship?
- In what areas of your life do you have a hard time telling the truth?
- When was the last time you were untruthful?
- What's your instinctive reaction when someone or something hurts you?
- What are you most hesitant to talk about regarding a committed relationship?
- What does freedom mean to you in a committed relationship?
- What is your definition of cheating?
- Have you ever cheated on someone?
- Have you ever been cheated on?
- What is your stance on monogamy?

- In a committed relationship, do you feel it is healthy or unhealthy to check to see if your partner is being faithful?
- Have you ever had to rebuild trust in a relationship?
- When your trust was broken, what steps did you take to restore it?
- Would you be willing to seek outside intervention for infidelity in a relationship?
- What is your definition of commitment?
- Are you ready to be in a committed relationship?
- How long does it take for you to know you're ready to be in a committed relationship?
- Are you, or have you ever been, afraid of commitment?
- What do you need from your potential partner to show they are committed to the relationship?
- How do you show you are committed to a relationship?
- If you are in a committed relationship, is it okay for your partner to look and not touch?
- When it comes to trust and commitment, do you believe that you and your potential partner need to be aligned?
- Have you ever stayed in a relationship when trust and commitment weren't aligned?
- How did your parents show their commitment, or lack of commitment, to each other? How, if at all, do you think their example influences you?
- Would your last partner say your word is good and you are faithful to your promises?

Notes

1-D: To Listen & To Share

More than anything, we need to be able to tell our partner what we are thinking and/or feeling. Communication is absolutely vital to a healthy relationship and honest communication helps to build trust.

You will ask questions to learn all you can about your partner and vice versa. You have to talk through likes, dislikes, bad habits, irritations, and pleasures. Basically, the good, the bad, and the ugly.

As we are all different, communicating these differences early on will help clear up misunderstandings later on. So what's the first step? You have to be open and honest. Chemistry and physical attraction will only get you so far. It's important to get the answers that may not be satisfactory as soon as you can. That way, you can make a decision or a compromise and then a choice based on what you've learned.

Today, there are several modes of communication, far more than ever before. Cell phones, with access to calls, texts, emails, dm's, posts, tweets, Facetime, Google Duo, WhatsApp, and guess what? There's still silence at times. We are well equipped to communicate on so many levels but at times we choose to give one another the silent treatment, or think the other person can read our minds.

You have to be comfortable to openly and honestly express your feelings with your partner. When communicating about something that's difficult, remaining calm is key. The goal of the conversation is to try to learn the other person's perspective, and see if common ground can be found or at least some kind of understanding. Now, this must be done without judgment or anger, and of course this is easier said than done. But when two people learn how to work as a team, they are in a much better position for this to happen. The goal is not to have a winner and a loser. But to be on the same team and come out stronger and better.

Now, just as important, and in many cases more important, is how we listen to our partner. A great deal of our time awake in a day, approximately 80%, is spent engaging in actually speaking and/or listening. That's way too much time to be doing something incorrectly or even inefficiently. In a relationship, not only do we want to be heard, we want to be understood.

In my work with couples, I realized that communication suffers because of their inability to listen to one another. Listening helps to demonstrate understanding, the desire for clarification or solving a problem or just enhancing the connection. This connectedness is key in an intentional relationship and is required to build a foundation. Without this foundation, you will be on shaky ground. Simply put, your relationship will not withstand challenges that inevitably arise.

As there are so many different modes of communication these days, the importance of face to face conversation is sometimes lost. Have you ever texted something that was completely misinterpreted? Remember, there are so many things that can be misconstrued via a text so be careful how you choose to communicate something important!

Les and I prefer the old-fashioned method of face to face

conversing. I have learned to ask Les for clarification when we are communicating if I don't understand or agree with what he is saying. I do this so I am not making any assumptions.

Les is a very calm person when he communicates. He is deliberate and I have learned that he chooses his words wisely. I tend to communicate the same way so that has been an area of strength for us. Conversations that would have fallen apart in the first five minutes with ex partners are able to be talked through and resolved. It has been the best feeling for both of us to have our feelings validated by the other. It has helped us to be more vulnerable, feel safer, and know that on the other side of a tough conversation, there is still love and a strong bond.

When finding that person for you, make sure you understand how they listen, how well they share, and how much of a team player they are in the realm of communication.

QUESTIONS TO ASK EACH OTHER

- How would you describe good/effective communication?
- Do you consider yourself to be a good communicator?
- Do you consider yourself to be a good listener?
- Do you believe being a good listener is important? Why or why not?
- Do you believe listening is a sign of affirmation?
- How important do you think communication is in a partnership?
- What kind of communication makes you feel loved?
- What kind of communication pushes you away?

- When is the best time to talk if there is a potential conflict?
- During a conflict, do you prefer to talk or text?
- During a conflict, are you a calm communicator or driven by emotion?
- Do you communicate with your hands?
- When communicating, do you ever raise your voice?
- What challenges have you had communicating with a previous partner?
- How can you be a better communicator?
- If something bothers you, do you like to discuss it right away or sit with it for a bit?
- Are there any topics that are off limits or make you feel uncomfortable?
- Do you communicate more by voice call, text, or email?
- Do you believe you and your potential partner should share the same communication style?
- How would you feel about a partner who preferred non-verbal (text or email) communication versus face-to-face?
- What are your top three favorite things to talk about?
- What are your three least favorite things to talk about?
- Before you make a call, do you rehearse what you are going to say?
- Do you seek to understand before being understood?
- Do you tend to give your partner "the silent treatment" when you have a disagreement?
- Have you ever been the recipient of "the silent treatment" and if so, how did you handle it?

Notes

1-E: Faith

"Religious wars are not caused by the fact that there is more than one religion, but by the spirit of intolerance."
—Montesquieu

When seeking a life partner, generally you want someone you can grow with mentally, physically, and spiritually. It's difficult to be in alignment with someone not because of a different set of spiritual beliefs, but rather if you are not open to respecting the differences that exist between the two of you.

In our Intentional Dating Model, it is never too soon to discuss religious beliefs. Acknowledging your beliefs and talking through differences with your partner is a MUST. Through healthy conversation, couples can evolve and learn each other better, differences and all. Avoidance of this topic is not sustainable for varying reasons and can later become a source of conflict and tension. Not to mention, many decisions you make in your relationship are influenced by your faith, i.e. sex before marriage, how children are raised, etc.

Keep in mind, religious differences can exist between couples of the same faith and this should be talked through as well. For example, church. How often, or at all, do both people think is necessary to attend a worship service?

Of course, there are different strokes for different folks. And spiritual growth can be achieved just from exposure to a different belief. Some couples learn from each other a different way to pray, a different way to incorporate the Bible in your spiritual journey, and this can go a long way. Making an effort to learn about your partner's faith is invaluable. Being intentional in this interest conveys a degree of love and acceptance. It tells our partner we value who they are and their beliefs, and although they are not ours, they are important to us.

If unable to accept your potential partner's beliefs that are not your own, refrain from making the mistake of going in with the intention of converting them. Wrong intention! Nothing can feel more invalidating than your significant other pointing out what is wrong with your belief system. At the end of the day, if your potential partner is not a good match because of their religious beliefs, how will you ever be a supportive partner? Couples have to address faith-based decisions that may not be compromisable at the start.

In addition, do not view conversion as your only solution. It is never recommended to try and convert your partner as a way to keep the peace throughout your relationship/marriage. This can create long-term resentment that becomes difficult to break through without professional help.

Another key point to remember is understanding the ways in which religious traditions are intertwined with many family traditions. If Christmas is a time for family but not celebrated by your partner, they may choose to be alone. How will this impact the two of you and possibly your children and extended family? It's important to have these conversations early as interference with those outside your nuclear family can create an even greater conflict.

Learn as much as you can about your partner's spiritual life and share more about yours. Sharing will also help your partner understand the deeper meaning it has for you. Discover any commonalities and don't forget, it is quite possible to love someone of a different faith and still be dedicated to your own.

QUESTIONS TO ASK EACH OTHER

- Do you consider yourself a religious or spiritual person? Why or why not?
- When did you choose your faith?
- Do you attend church?
- Do you think someone needs to attend church to be spiritual?
- Did you have to change your life before you started following a religion?
- Do you believe in God or a higher being?
- Can someone believe in God but not attend church?
- What should a believer do before they die?
- Were you raised in any particular religion?
- Where in your life are you religious and why?
- What do you have absolute faith in?
- What are the daily rituals you swear by and think everyone else should consider?
- Do you believe in heaven and hell?
- What misconceptions are there about faith?
- Do you believe in prayer?
- What's your favorite prayer?
- What are your feelings about a couple who don't share the

same spiritual beliefs?

- Would you date someone with a different religious background than you? Why or why not?
- How would your family feel if your significant other had a different religion?
- Why do bad things happen to good people?
- What can younger generations get out of religion?
- How will you handle religion and your children?
- What is the last spiritual book you read?
- Have you read the Bible?
- Do you have a favorite book/chapter in the Bible?

Notes

_____

_____

_____

_____

_____

_____

_____

_____

_____

_____

1-F: Evenly Yoked

Moving at a similar pace and cadence, being in sync. This is sometimes referred to as "being evenly yoked" and it is important in a long-term romantic relationship. They say opposites attract but dating someone with more similarities than not can promote better understanding which can lead to more satisfaction.

Differences can spice things up, but when two people's core values are aligned, research has found that they are more compatible over time. This in no way suggests you have to find someone just like you. We want you to make sure their walk is just as intentional as yours. We want the two of you to embrace your differences and cultivate it into your relationship.

Overcompensating or lowering one's standards are just a few potential outcomes when choosing someone who isn't compatible with you. As an illustration, have you ever had an injury to one knee and in order to not distress that knee, you put additional pressure on the good knee? In the end, both knees are messed up! Same goes for this situation. Putting uneven pressure on yourself or your partner is no different, in the end, as you both will suffer.

This is not about a formal education, although it could be. This is about you and your partner's similarities when it comes to your quest of knowledge, goal achievement, and drive.

I spent some time wanting to inspire a gentleman I was involved with to standardize his business operations so he could use his time more efficiently to grow. On several occasions when we discussed goals, it felt like we were both on the same page, but when it came to execution, he met me with resistance which caused a great deal of tension and conflict. We both had goals but our ways of pursuing them were very different. Looking back, I was continually trying to fit a round peg into a square hole as opposed to accepting our obvious differences. Then determining whether or not those differences in this area (and others), would jeopardize our sustainability.

His desire to do things the way they had always been done and my continual push to introduce new ideas and strategies, became a great divide in our day to day lives. He ultimately resented me and I grew more and more frustrated. This pattern ensued and to my dismay, talking through these, and other, issues wasn't an option either due to communication differences so we remained stuck. In our case, our very different backgrounds were part of the initial attraction but the lack of commonality in our core values ultimately led to our demise.

Les believed that his partner in a previous relationship seemed intimidated by his college friends. After a couple of trips to visit his alma mater, she made it clear that she had no interest in those social interactions. It could have been a result of their greatly varying life experiences, what she had been and had not been exposed to both educationally and culturally.

My goals and Les' goals and work-related pursuits are more alike than different. We recognized that towards the beginning and it has helped in so many ways. We are very understanding of each other's work schedule, often one working just as late as the other (SMH)! We seldom get tired of learning, planning, and executing. We have very similar drives, and put similar amounts of energy into making our dreams a reality. We both like the reference POWER COUPLE but our expectations of what it realistically takes to get there is aligned too, thankfully.

QUESTIONS TO ASK EACH OTHER

- What is your definition of intelligence?
- When choosing a partner, is their intellect a primary consideration?
- How important is intellectual stimulation for you in a relationship?
- Does it matter if there is a difference in educational backgrounds?
- Will your family have difficulty accepting your potential partner if they are less educated than you are?
- Would you be comfortable with a partner whose educational accomplishments exceed yours?
- What are/were your educational goals? What have you done to achieve them?
- What is your current daily schedule (school or work)?
- How could this schedule impact our time together?
- Do you or did you attend college?
- How important is higher education to you?
- What challenges have you faced with school?
- Do you equate more education to higher earnings?
- Have you been able to complete your educational goals? If not, what were your barriers?

- What fields interest you?
- What fields bore you?
- If you could have the answer to any one question, what question would you want the answer to?
- If you could instantly receive a PhD in any discipline (both knowledge and experience), what would the PhD be in?
- Where are you playing it too safe in your pursuit of higher education?
- What's the accomplishment you are most proud of?
- What is something you have yet to accomplish?
- What makes you get out of bed in the morning?
- What prevents you from getting out of bed in the morning?
- What part of your daily routine do you most look forward to every day?
- What book had the most impact on you as a child?
- What is your favorite book today?
- What is the last book you read?
- What class or teacher had the most impact on your life growing up?

Notes

_____

_____

_____

_____

_____

1-G: Making Our Work, Work!

Work Hard, Play Harder!

According to a recent Gallop poll, over 25% of people are "somewhat or completely dissatisfied with their stress at work." This means one out of four of your friends are having some or many bad work days! Even if it's just some, the impact of bad days can have negative consequences and easily spill over into the home environment.

Let's say your partner returns home from work in a negative space, feeling agitated, frustrated, or even defeated. How will their mood impact you? Will their stress become your stress if they are short with you or argumentative, or even less affectionate?

Our partners can be a sounding board for us to talk through our work problems, a safe space to vent and figure out solutions. But when stressed, sometimes they miss these opportunities.

When choosing your partner, ask questions about their work, their job satisfaction, and their stress level. Find out how they handle on-the-job stress. Are they able to detach from the work day and be present at home? This is especially true for someone in a leadership capacity, with endless responsibility and accountability. Can they leave work at work to come home and truly focus on their partner?

What about now, in a world where the COVID-19 pandemic completely changed how we live, where we work, and how we work. Couples who were used to leaving the home for nine to ten hours a day were suddenly working remotely, navigating through their day in the same space with their significant other. That's a major adjustment and must be considered when evaluating a potential partner. If we live together and are both working from home, how will it impact us as a team? Being with someone who is able to communicate their needs, wants, what is working and what's not working is necessary. A relationship check-in can be extremely helpful during these particular times where things are constantly changing. Talk about what worked yesterday and what didn't and what needs to be done differently tomorrow.

Or, what if you're dating an entrepreneur! Les has had his own company since 2011. He may make it look easy, but in no means is it or has it ever been. Of course, there is a degree of freedom, no corporate work schedule in which to adhere, no PTO, no unreasonable bosses and a degree of flexibility. But, due to great discipline, Les is still at his desk at the same time every morning, day after day, getting it done. He works long hours during the week but is always ready for our Friday date night, a Saturday activity, and our cozy Sunday routine. He has had great success as a CEO but not without his share of challenges. As an entrepreneur, he has had to work tirelessly creating different networks to offer his products and services. He sits in front of the right people many times, and there are still no guarantees. At times, he has become discouraged because he's human. However, he has been able to separate the business demands from our relationship.

What he told me early on and has demonstrated through his actions is that OUR MARRIAGE comes first. I don't have to feel secondary to his business. Knowing that, I can be his biggest cheerleader. I celebrate the big deals and talk through the missed opportunities. We are able to have open, honest, and vulnerable conversations around work and our finances. Instead of hiding our concerns with work, or our fears, we share them and face them together.

Regardless of your job situation, do not wait to discuss what your routine will be, ways you will make time for each other, how you will incorporate your date nights, prayers, and/or your family activities with the children. If prioritizing your family needs comes first, be sure you align with someone who shares those same values. Harmony will increase tenfold as the two of you have a healthy balance of work and living. Les and I both work hard but we play even harder. We travel monthly, plan long weekend excursions, and look forward to going everywhere on our bucket lists.

Stay mindful, respectful, and supportive of each other's career pursuits. That's how we started operating early. There is nothing more attractive to Les than when I support and encourage his vision and vice versa. As work-related things happen around us, one thing that remains constant is our deliberate team approach.

We were able to figure out how to make our work, work. You can do this too when starting an intentional journey by communicating early, honestly, and openly.

QUESTIONS TO ASK EACH OTHER

- Are you currently working?
- Do you enjoy what you do professionally?
- What would be your dream job?

- What has prevented you from obtaining your dream job?
- Where do you see yourself in five years? Ten years?
- What would you do if you had enough money not to need a job?
- What would you do for work, even if you weren't paid for it?
- Do you prefer to work in a team or alone?
- Where would you move if you could move anywhere in the world and still find a job and maintain a reasonable standard of living?
- What skills have you always wanted to learn?
- Other than financial rewards, what else have you gained in your current work?
- Is it possible for anyone to be completely self-made?
- Do you think it's ever possible to be an overnight success?
- What's something most people haven't done career-wise but you have?
- What's the best or worse job you have had?
- What's the hardest you've worked for something?
- Where are you falling short of your potential?
- What's your go-to strategy for achieving your goals?
- Where in your life are you lazy and what's your excuse?
- Where would you like to retire?
- What does an average work week look like for you?
- What about your job makes you want to get up in the morning?
- How do you feel about entrepreneurialism?

- How comfortable are you with taking risks?
- Have you ever started a business?
- Have you been successful at running a business?
- What are you most proud of professionally?
- Who or what inspires you in your career?
- Do you get along with your coworkers?
- How have you gotten along with supervisors?
- Have you had any conflict at work?
- At what age do you want to retire?
- Are you a planner or spontaneous person?
- What is the most attractive industry to you?
- What is something an outsider would not know about your industry?
- Is there a job you would never do?
- What's the first thing you do after getting home from work?
- How do you approach taking time off from work?
- Do you have a long commute to work?
- Are you able to work from home?
- Has the pandemic changed what you do for work?
- Do you believe a couple can be in business together successfully?
- At work, are you a risk taker or do you tend to play it safe?

Notes

1-H: Screen Time

THIS CHAPTER RIGHT HERE! We could write an entire book on this topic, but for now we are going to briefly discuss our perspectives as well as a few common challenges we found with these necessary devices.

In our relationships, we have freely given our partners:
- keys to our cars
- keys to our houses
- kids (to take care of)
- bodies (intimacy)
- credit & debit cards

But have you freely given your partner the passcode to your social media accounts and cell phone? If you haven't, why not? If you trust your partner to take care of your kids, and you co-sign for their car, and have joint bank accounts with them, why don't you trust them enough to share your social media and/or phone passcodes with them?

Privacy

Yes, we are all entitled to privacy. But when you're married, shouldn't your spouse have your sensitive information in case of an emergency?

When I first started dating Les, I realized he was a daily Facebook poster which was different from myself. I questioned some of his posts, unsure of what the purpose was, and because I lived a more private life. We had some conversations about my anxiety around his being more public, and how I would handle that. We decided to discuss parameters around posting so both parties felt comfortable and have minimized our challenges as a result.

These are our recommendations on how you can make social media, texting, and cell phones function in your relationship, and also minimize drama:

1. **Be open with your partner and discuss how you want to handle social media, texting, and cell phones.** Share what is acceptable for you as well as which apps/sites are not acceptable to use if you are in a committed relationship. Listen to your partner's thoughts on how and why they use their social media pages, text, and other phone apps.

2. **Be honest if you saw something online or on the cell phone that bothers you.** For example, if you see an alert from an app that is on the "not acceptable" list pop-up on your partner's phone—who has agreed to be exclusive—talk to them directly and without judgment as soon as possible instead of letting it fester over a long period of time. Whether you were the one who saw the notification or the person who received it, an open and blameless discussion can help both of you better understand each other and what the notification was about.

3. **Be aware that using emojis or small gestures can take on unintentional or bigger meanings.** What does it mean

when you or your partner comments, likes, loves, or better yet, responds with an emoji on a photo or accepts a friend request from an attractive person they say that they don't know? It's important to acknowledge that these types of responses can mean a wide range of intentions (or not), and it would be helpful to have a proactive and direct conversation.

I remember a fight I had in a previous relationship that started like this. "Oh, so you're writing comments with emojis and shit on these females' pages!? You barely like or comment on any of my post!!" Yeah, it was an innocent smiley face but it caused a long few days. Let's do our best to avoid situations like this.

4. **Recognize that some folks study your pages so be intentional with what you share. What and how you post doesn't merely impact you. It can impact others in your circle, especially your partner.** Posting on social media isn't often what it seems, leaving things to be misconstrued. As this can impact a partner's feelings and reactions in a very real way, it's important not to minimize or downplay your partner's feelings or response. I didn't understand how many people pay attention to your social media posts and assume it to be your current reality (and question whether you're living what you are posting). I have even looked at others' posts and have been guilty of wondering things like, "Is she still married? I don't see her posting any pictures of her husband. I wonder what's up with that."

When looking at her husband's page, I noticed his posts told a different story. If they are in agreement with these optics, all is well. However, if not, discussing your partner's desires around what & how you post is key. Although two people can have unique posting styles, the content and meaning, and ultimately the respect for one another, should be aligned. It is our goal to have our readers not leave any ambiguity on their pages. Proudly let your followers know you are an intentional and unstoppable team.

5. **Realize there may be deeper issues at work here. Deeper than social media posts, texting, or using certain apps.** If you find your or your partner's use of any of these items makes either of you uncomfortable, please recognize each other's feelings and spend some time discussing the potential reasons. Most of the time, these feelings come from issues that were in previous relationships and are often related to trust and commitment. Another reason could be the lack of quality time you two spend together in your current relationship.

6. **Granny's #1 rule aka "The Golden Rule."** Treat others as you want to be treated.

QUESTIONS TO ASK EACH OTHER

- How well do you cope when you don't have your phone with you for an extended period of time?
- What's your favorite app on your phone?

- What's the phone app you use the most?
- What's your social media weakness?
- What social media account has taught you the most?
- If you gave up all of your social media accounts, how would your life be better? How would your life be worse?
- Has any particular app caused a problem in previous relationships?
- Do you prefer your partner to put their phone face up or face down? Why?
- Have you ever given your partner your password?
- Do you believe you should have your partner's password?
- How do you feel about your partner on social media?
- Are you a frequent poster?
- How do you feel about your partner posting?
- Is it important to announce your dating status on your social media pages?
- Should partners check in with each other before posting?
- How do you feel about your partner having a single status if the two of you are in a relationship?
- How do you feel about your partner still being friends with an ex?
- How do you feel about your partner commenting on others' pages?
- How do you feel about your partner being on their phone in bed before going to sleep?
- What bothers you the most about social media?
- Do you compare yourself to others on any social media

platform?

- Is anything that happens online reason enough to end a relationship?
- Do you ask permission before you post your partner on your page?
- Would you want your partner to ask your permission before posting on their page?
- Do you give your partner the benefit of the doubt about their posting?
- What is an absolute NO regarding social media posts while in a relationship?

Notes

_____

_____

_____

_____

_____

_____

_____

_____

_____

1-I: Open Wounds & Guarded Hearts

When pursuing an intentional journey, in addition to seeking the right choice, you have to *be* the right choice. For someone to make an informed decision about whether or not you are the one, they need to know who you are and from where you have come. In an aligned relationship, both partners must accept each other's past—the good, the bad, and the ugly—and be willing to embrace the future, history and all.

Syd and I definitely brought into our relationship issues stemming from past relationships and insecurities. We both had been in marriages where there had been infidelity and relationships in which there was a lack of open, honest, and transparent interaction. We still had very open wounds and guarded hearts. Although difficult, on our journey of intentionality, we understood the necessity of sharing.

When I first met Les, I was under tremendous stress dealing with some gut-wrenching challenges that caused a huge toll on my immediate family. Les made it clear about his intentionality, regardless of what problems or difficulties I had going on, but still I was uneasy. I did not want to share my full story in our beginning stages, but I knew I had to because we had made the decision to be intentional. On this very intentional journey, we had to make deliberate choices on purpose based on what was important to each of us. In this case, finding compatibility.

Living intentionally requires digging deep, making your mind up about actions you will take and then living them. How could Les make a deliberate choice and not know about something that was impacting me?

I had to share a part of my past and I did. I told my story walking across the Woodrow Wilson Bridge in December 2020. What I revealed was met with understanding and support. Instead of regretting my decision, it further confirmed Les' genuine desire to be a team, despite the challenges that lie ahead. He was willing to be in the trenches with me. I was not alone. His only request was that we go through it together. That was a pivotal moment for me.

Syd was especially understanding of my issues with actual or perceived cell phone shade. In a previous relationship, an ex had another life completely hidden on a device. This single 2" X 5" device told the gigantic stories engulfed in lies, deception, and betrayal and it was a huge blow to my ego when discovered. When I met Syd, that pain was still there and in one of our early conversations where I was vulnerable, I shared the details. Instead of highlighting this as a negative, she was able to provide reassurances that we all have a past and despite the inevitable traces we may bring from them, she would have my back. I knew then that I'd found a true partner who was willing to move forward despite her baggage and mine.

QUESTIONS TO ASK EACH OTHER

- Are you ashamed about anything from your past?
- What in your past has made it hard to date?
- What in your past has helped you in the early phases of a relationship?
- What is something you would like to overcome from your past?

- What events in your past are you too scared to talk about?
- What was missing from your childhood?
- In what ways are you most different from the person you were in high school?
- What did you used to enjoy doing as a child that is no longer part of your life?
- How easy is it for you to lose your temper and why?
- What's the best mistake you ever made and why?
- What decision are you grateful you didn't make?
- What's something you'd be embarrassed for me to know?
- What bridges are you happy you have burned?
- What's the most valuable lesson you learned from your past relationship?
- When was the last time you cried in front of someone?
- How many serious relationships have you been in?
- When was your first kiss?
- When did you lose your virginity?
- Is there anything you regret doing or not doing in a past relationship?
- How did your past relationship end?
- Have you ever been in an open relationship?
- What happened on your worst date?
- What happened on your best date?
- Who in your life do you wish you met sooner?
- What lesson are you most thankful you learned in your past?
- Do you believe your past has contributed to who you are today?

- In what way(s) are you a different person than you were ten years ago?
- What were some of the turning points in your life?
- When was the first time you said "I love you" to someone who isn't a member of your family?
- What have been the highest and lowest points of your life?
- If you could apologize to one person from your past, who would it be and why?

Notes

_____

_____

_____

_____

_____

_____

_____

_____

_____

_____

_____

_____

_____

STEP 2: Dates 4 – 6
"My Circle of Life"

2-A: Accountability Circle

When you're transitioning into an intentional courtship, more than in previous relationships, you'll need a strong inner-circle. A small tight-knit group that will a) support your relationship goal, b) keep you accountable (to yourself and your non-negotiables), and c) encourage you throughout the journey.

I've always maintained at least four types of friends in my inner-circle. Occasionally, you may have one or two friends that fill multiple types and/or alternate their roles. My inner-circle has at least one of these types of friends in it constantly:

The Loyal Best Friend
This is the friend that keeps you sane. They are your non-judgmental and your most supportive ally. They keep your secrets and know where the bodies are buried but still have an unshakable love for you.

The Keep It 100 Confidant
When you need to hear/know the 1000% truth about anything, they have no problem telling it to you. Sometimes you wonder if they get some "low-key" joy from being so straight with you (lol). But seriously, take their direct words constructively, and move accordingly. Today's world is full of "yes men" but for this journey, you need a brutally honest friend.

The Wise O.G.

Nipsey Hussle said, "If you look at the people in your circle and you do not get inspired, then you don't have a circle, you have a cage." You need to have a friend in your circle that challenges you to be the best version of yourself at all times, especially when no one else is around. They guide you to be patient and wise, all the time moving toward your goal. This mentor friend is usually older and a few life experiences ahead of you. Generally, you desire to be like them.

The Fixer/Enforcer

This friend type is not pertinent to this discussion, but is on my list (transparency). In his song Never Change from The Blueprint, Jay-Z says, "I'd never mention your name, I promise respect. Death before dishonor, correct? Plead the fifth when it comes to the fam, I'm like a dog, I never speak, but I understand."

Simply put, this is the friend that appears when you have an issue that needs attention, adjustment, or correction. Their motto is, "Say less."

My best friend Erik and I have been "brothas" since his family moved from New York to my neighborhood "D-Block" in 1972. He has witnessed or knew of most, if not all, of my relationships. After my second divorce, we spent an incredible amount of time evaluating the entire relationship from its fun start to its Hindenburg-ish end. After spending some much needed time on myself, I shared my written non-negotiables list, and he understood why each of them would be key to the success of my next marriage being my best marriage.

Lately, Erik also has served as my keep it 100 confidant, too. So once I shared my non-negotiables with him, he loved keeping me accountable to it. He consistently asked me the difficult questions that forced me to remain true to my "chosen path" if I showed any signs of wavering. He recognized when I was getting off track and bending my non-negotiables due to maybe having some relational history, lust, or status. Knowing this, he would use his "rubber mallet" (hard, but not damaging) to ask questions and provoke thoughts to allow me to reign myself back onto the path.

My wise O.G. is my brother-in-law Herman (Herm). Herm has been in my life since I was a kid. He married my sister when I was eight years old and was the big brother my biological big brother couldn't be (this is another story, for another time). I looked up to my dad but Herm was/is my "tangible" role model. Every little boy wanted to have a big brother that was a college athlete like Herm. He was highly respected and influential in his career. He was popular, active, and respected in our community. He was an impeccable husband to my sister and today he continues to be a great father to my nieces. I know I don't know everything that went on or what they've gone through as a couple, but not once did I ever hear my sister, my mother, my dad, or anyone in the street say anything negative about Herm or what type of father he was to my nieces, or what type of husband he was to my sister. I strived (and failed), and still strive to have this type of private and public record when it comes to being a father and a husband.

When I shared with Herm the journey I was about to start, he reminded me not to be distracted by looks and/or money and most importantly, to be transparent with your potential partner about EVERYTHING. He was gently reminding me that I have had a busy history and my future wife should know about all aspects of it.

He and my dad are/were firm believers in total transparency and letting a potential spouse know exactly what you desire & require. Then let them make the informed decision to choose you as their spouse. I not only live by this guidance but I share it as often as I can.

My sister became ill in 2014 and Herm remained consistently by her side—truly in sickness and in health—until the day she joined our ancestors in early 2020. Herm is and has been a man of few words. He is the embodiment of letting your actions speak for you. So when he does speak, I listen closely and take heed. I strive every day to be the father, husband, and mentor he has been.

So I implore you to surround yourself with hard, firm, loving, truthful, intelligent, seasoned, and God-fearing friends. They will be the reason you will stay the course and be the "first and best" choice for your potential spouse.

QUESTIONS TO ASK EACH OTHER

- Who are your kind of people?
- How did you meet your best friend?
- What's the most essential part of a friendship?

- What's the strangest way you've become friends with someone?
- What's the best way to know who someone really is?
- How different do you act when you are with acquaintances versus people you are comfortable with?
- What friendship have you had with the most impact?
- Among your friends, what are you best known for?
- Who is the strongest person you know and how do you wish you were more like them?
- Which friend would you call to help you bury the body and why?
- How has peer pressure shaped your life?
- Whose marriage do you consider to be a model marriage and why?
- Who else do you count on as a source of support?
- Do you have more same sex friends or friends of the opposite sex?
- Are you able to set healthy boundaries with your friends?
- Do you argue with your friends a lot?
- Do you have a small circle, medium circle, or large circle?
- Do you tell your friends all your secrets?
- When do you introduce someone you are dating to your friends?
- Who is your oldest friend?
- Would you tell your significant other your best friend's secrets?
- Do your friends hold you accountable and if so, how?

- Do you hold your friends accountable?
- Do you spend more time alone or with friends?
- Do you like to double date with friends?
- Are most of your friends married or single?
- Are you a jealous person?
- Are you envious of any of your friends?
- What qualities are you most attracted to in a friend?
- Have you ever crossed the line intimately with a close friend?

Notes

_____

_____

_____

_____

_____

_____

_____

_____

_____

_____

2-B: All In The Family

When Les and I began our premarital counseling, one thing in particular our pastor said was not only are you marrying your potential partner, you are marrying their family as well. He clarified stating that families are an extension of us and you cannot separate your spouse from the family they came from. If there were certain dynamics in the home environment that your potential partner was raised in, for instance if they came from a home in which communication wasn't great, those issues might resurface in your household. Take time during the beginning phase to discuss your family relationships, how different family members treated one another, and how conflict was handled. All this matters as no family is perfect.

Les grew up with both his parents, two older siblings and his grandmother. I grew up as an only child raised by a single mother. It was no surprise that we had very different childhood experiences. Although my nuclear family was small, Thanksgiving and Christmas dinners were spent with extended family making these days very large gatherings. Although Les' nuclear family was much larger, holiday celebrations were much smaller. I checked in with Les early on to find out if we were to move forward, would he be comfortable with larger family events around the holidays. Similarly, he checked in with me to find out if I would be open to traveling alone together on occasion during the holiday season. We decided that we would both have to compromise to allow the other their preferences around these significant days.

Although Les and I reconnected later in life, and once our

children were young adults, we still had to consider how our being together would impact our relationships with each other's children. For us, this was less difficult because our children were older. But it was still an important area for us since we both value family. We weren't sure how things would pan out initially, but we talked through our needs and desires, and planned our initial meetings once we were clear that we were going to be in a committed relationship.

In the getting-to-know-you phase, as you are entering into a relationship with someone who has been married before or shares a child with someone, there could be many situations that present themselves. Perhaps there's a toxic relationship with an ex, a love-hate relationship with a mother, or an estrangement from a parent. Whatever the case, what's most important is that there is an understanding that you two will make every effort to not let these issues impact your relationship and you remain a team that chooses to face these challenges together.

Les was willing to accept some of the family challenges I had going on with my youngest child and I was willing to be supportive as he rehabilitated a relationship with his daughters after a traumatizing divorce. We both were there for each other, listening and remaining non-judgmental.

QUESTIONS TO ASK EACH OTHER

- What is your family's cultural background?
- Do you have any children? If so, how many? What are their ages?

- If no children, do you want to have children? If so, how many?
- If you do not want children, why?
- Do your children live with you?
- Would you give your child more or less freedom than you had growing up?
- How do you feel about adult children living at home?
- What key life advice did you learn from your children?
- What dreams do you have for your children? Grandchildren?
- How do you feel children should be disciplined?
- What's one thing you want to do or wished you had done before having children?
- Are your parents living or deceased?
- Describe your relationship with your mother in one sentence.
- Describe your relationship with your father in one sentence?
- In what ways are you like your parents?
- Were your parents married? If so, what did you observe about their marriage?
- Was divorce a part of your family?
- How did your family resolve conflict when you were growing up?
- What's the best advice you received from your parents?
- How many siblings do you have?
- What is your relationship like with each of your siblings?
- How important are your siblings to you?

- Where does your immediate family reside?
- Where would your family be most surprised to find you?
- Which family member are you most grateful for?
- Who is the person in your family that you are the most honest with?
- What's the thing you most hope to replicate from your own upbringing?
- In three words, how would you describe your childhood?
- What one value defines your family the most?
- What's your favorite family tradition?
- What is the most unique family tradition of your family?
- Is it important that you are with your family during the holidays?
- Is it important for your family to accept your significant other?
- Do you make your partner a priority when with your family? If yes, how?
- If you could change one thing about the way you were raised, what would it be and why?
- How does your family express love and affection?
- What is your expectation of your partner's treatment of your family?

Notes

2-C: Time Won't Give Me Time

"Time is the most precious gift you can give to someone, because if you give someone your time… it's a part of your life that you will never get back."
—Gloria Tesch

Time is the most valuable asset we possess. Once you spend it, you will never get it back, so make wise decisions about who you spend time with and be mindful of others' time. To me, not respecting my time is as disrespectful as slapping my mother!

People will show you how important you are to them based on how they respect or value your time. Identifying early similarities and differences with respect to time management is a key factor in the ultimate success or demise of a relationship.

Les and I discovered early that we held our daily planners and routines in high regard. Managing time was so important to each of us and a top priority. We enjoyed planning our days and weekends, and it has made life easier. But this has not always been the case in some of our prior relationships.

We both have dated people who didn't respect time, didn't plan for the day, let alone make long-term plans. Although it didn't work well with us, we realize this doesn't always have to negatively impact the relationship. It only happens when there are different approaches and perspectives when it comes to time and one person is rigid, and wants the other to adopt their approach.

If your partner is okay with running red lights and running in airports instead of allocating the needed time and proper planning, and you know this will get under your skin, discuss how you will manage these types of situations. Effectively compromising is a golden rule in any relationship and if this is an area in which compromise cannot be achieved, long-term compatibility may be in question.

QUESTIONS TO ASK EACH OTHER

- Do you value time?
- Do you tend to arrive early, be on time, or arrive fashionably late?
- Do you expect your partner to be on time?
- How would you resolve time issues with your partner?
- Do you have any daily time constraints?
- Do you consider yourself to be an organized person?
- How do you prioritize tasks?
- How do you manage deadlines?
- Do you think it is important to manage your time well?
- How do you balance work and personal life?
- What tools do you use to manage time?
- What is your ideal timeframe to get to know someone before becoming serious?
- In a relationship, how important is quality time?
- If your partner wanted more time, could you accommodate their request?
- Besides home and work, where do you spend most of your time?

- What is more important to you, time or money? Why?
- How much time is enough time with your partner?
- How much time is too little time with your partner?
- Do you like to spend more time alone or together?
- What do you think is the biggest waste of time?

Notes

_____

_____

_____

_____

_____

_____

_____

_____

_____

_____

_____

_____

_____

_____

2-D: Bankrupting Relationships

"Money may not buy love but fighting about it will bankrupt your relationship."

I don't know who needs to hear this but someone's salary alone won't make it work. Don't equate one's earning potential with whether or not they are a good choice for you.

There are plenty of financially set couples who aren't happy. Yes, paying bills is not an area of concern, but perhaps loneliness, isolation, and emotional bankruptcy are. Some couples have expressed that as their income grew, so did their divide. There are also couples with money who still argue over it. Money is money, whether hundreds, thousands, or hundreds of thousands.

Wealth can secure a couple a comfortable lifestyle but does not guarantee what matters most as you grow older together—intimacy, respect, healthy communication, and true love.

It's a great feeling when love and financial stability coexist, and when there's one and not the other, here comes trouble. Love cannot live without money. And money without love can't live. At least not in today's time.

Partners should strive to become involved with someone who has a similar idea of financial responsibility. Remember, financial situations can change. In life, there is a cost to everything and money is needed to sustain a living. Choose a partner who understands that financial security is tied to choices, hustle, responsible spending, and consistent saving/investment.

Or consider the person who depends solely on their partner

financially. At one point, they may be torn when it comes to spending. What is too much and will it be met with contention? Why do I need to ask to spend a certain amount if we are together? What are my limits and should I have a limit? The answers to these questions should be clear so any decisions around spending aren't costing peace and robbing happiness.

Love is difficult when one has no money, no matter who you are. As you're preparing for an intentional journey, get your finances in order. Position yourself to make money and make that money work for you. Enter into a relationship with intentions of getting your credit in order, with the ability to contribute and feel empowered by your own financial decision making. Some of the financial matters that should be asked and answered include:

- Credit
- Spending habits
- Saving habits
- Overall money management

One person's negative habits can have a detrimental effect on a relationship including inability to contribute to the household, inability to secure capital, ongoing financial stress, and eventually a delayed retirement. Financial compatibility plays a huge role in your relationship's long-term success.

QUESTIONS TO ASK EACH OTHER

- What is more important, money or success?
- Do you believe money can buy happiness?

- Is it important for your partner to make the same amount of money as you?
- Would you be comfortable if your spouse/partner didn't manage money well?
- Are you a saver or a spender?
- At what age should you start saving?
- Do you own any stocks/bonds?
- Do you have any investments outside of stocks and bonds?
- What is the definition of financial security/stability to you?
- Do you have a personal checking account?
- What is your credit score?
- Do you have any judgements or garnishments against you?
- Have you ever filed bankruptcy?
- Do you pay or receive child support?
- Are you current with your state and federal tax returns?
- What's really expensive but totally worth it?
- If you unexpectedly won a million dollars, what would you spend it on?
- In what ways are you bad with money?
- How did your parents influence your relationship with money?

Notes

2-E: Netflix or The Game

How couples spend their free time together is also paramount in a relationship. Each person in a partnership is likely to have interests they may enjoy more than the other. This is okay as long as there is priority placed on engaging in some mutually enjoyed activities together. For example, your spouse may enjoy binge watching Netflix shows while you may have difficulty sitting through one episode. What's a fair compromise in this scenario?

The ways that couples handle their alone time versus time together can make or break their relationship. Frequent messages heard in couple's counseling are that quality time is lacking, all they want to do is XYZ, or we are in the same space but living different lives. Identify common interests and hobbies and be intentional about doing them together as these are the things you will do as friends and being friends allows your love to grow.

Having a partner but feeling alone is very disheartening and is often a precursor to misery and feelings of neglect and rejection. Prevent this by intentionally evaluating compatibility with regards to interests and hobbies. Ask identifying questions to understand and determine compatibility in how each of you spend your free time alone and how you envision spending free time together is very important. Discussing areas such as these can prevent differences down the line. The earlier you know about these (and other) behaviors and preferences, the better off your future will be.

QUESTIONS TO ASK EACH OTHER

- What was the best party (concert) you've ever attended?
- How often do you dance?
- What song always gets you out onto the dance floor?
- Do you play a musical instrument? If so, which one?
- Do you enjoy sports? If so, what is your favorite sport?
- What is your favorite team?
- Who is your favorite player?
- What are some movies you really enjoyed?
- What was the last book you really got into?
- What do you like to do in your free time?
- Who is your favorite actor and/or actress?
- Who is your favorite character from a TV show, movie, or book?
- What TV or movie marital couple do you see yourself most like in your future?
- What types of movies (TV shows) do you like to watch?
- What was the last show you binge-watched?
- What's your go-to series or movie when you want to watch something but can't find anything to watch?
- Do you play video games? If so, what is your favorite game and why?
- What would you do with the extra time if you never had to sleep?
- What are you always game for?
- What do you do to unwind?

- What hobbies would you like to get into if you had the time and money?
- What's the most ridiculous thing you've done because you were bored?
- What's your favorite thing to do outdoors? Indoors?
- What do you like but are kinda embarrassed to admit?
- What do you wish we could spend more time on?
- What kinds of activities bore you?
- In your last relationship, what kind of activities did you like to do together?
- Do you believe someone can over-indulge in a hobby?
- How do you feel about your partner participating in an activity without you?
- Is it important for you to engage in a hobby with your partner?

Notes

_____

_____

_____

_____

_____

_____

_____

2-F: Beyond Superficial

We all know what "fine" and/or handsome is to us. You don't need our help to determine who is or who ain't sexy. What we are here to do is assist you with going beyond one's current appearance/attractiveness to get to the required traits of that person to establish a long-lasting relationship/marriage. When you really think about it, appearance should be equal to what the whipped cream is to a milkshake—a flavor bonus. Nothing more, nothing less. The milkshake is the primary treat, and the whipped cream is mainly there for decoration. I doubt you would trade the milkshake for only the whipped cream. Unfortunately, many of us do just that and then wonder why our "treat" has no substance to it and doesn't fill us up. Don't fall for the fluff!

In my own experience, I have seen many people miss the right person because they were too focused on outward appearances (whipped cream) versus all the other attributes (milkshake) that person brought to the table. Then twenty years later, they come to me and say, "Damn, I missed out on that good man/woman!" Don't miss the right person because they are not as fine or handsome as your ideal partner is in your mind. Please remember that external looks will fade over time, so don't overlook the qualified person that doesn't have a picture-perfect exterior. They may just be the right person that you need to be your partner in life. This partner will not only love you the way you need to be loved, but also provide you with all of the non-negotiables you require. Also, some folks are late bloomers so don't sleep! "I was that song you skipped, and found out later it was fire!"

QUESTIONS TO ASK EACH OTHER

- What role does physical attraction play in whether or not you pursue a relationship?
- Do you feel attractive? What do you like about the way you look?
- Is physical beauty a key to your happiness?
- Would you say you have a type? Do I fit what you thought you were looking for?
- What is the first thing you think when you see me?
- What is my most attractive quality?
- What is the first thing you noticed about me?
- What was the first thing you thought when you met me?
- What characteristics do you find least attractive in another person?
- What makes someone attractive to you?
- Which do you find more attractive, physical beauty or a good personality?
- Do you worry about how your looks and your partner's looks will change over time?
- Would you rather dress up or wear casual clothes?
- How important is style and fashion to you?
- If you didn't like something your partner was wearing, would you tell them?
- If you didn't like the way your partner wore their hair, would you tell them?
- How would you handle it if your partner gained or lost a

lot of weight?

- How would you handle it if your partner became disfigured as the result of an accident?
- How do you feel about tattoos? Do you have any?
- How do you feel about piercings? Do you have any?

Notes

_____

_____

_____

_____

_____

_____

_____

_____

_____

_____

_____

_____

_____

STEP 3: Dates 7 – 9
"My Future"

3-A: Date Night

According to the Urban Dictionary, "Romance" is a state of connection between two people that is brought about by thoughtful, sentimental gestures that mean something to one or both parties. These gestures communicate care, understanding and love as well as a desire to reach out and connect through the heart with a partner.

Let's revisit *The Five Love Languages* as we attempt to understand how our potential partner defines romance. A man or woman may perceive an evening of romance as dining at a high-end restaurant with sparkling wine in an effort to express love and admiration. Another may deem that cooking dinner at home and eating by candlelight is more romantic. Guess what? They are both right! Romance is subjective and can differ greatly from one person to the next. Therefore, it's important to identify its individual meaning early.

Taking time to identify your own romance definition as well as your partner's sets the stage for future appreciation, fulfillment, and a loving connection. Although it may feel awkward to ask a question in which you'd rather demonstrate your knowledge of, it's best to do so and be accurate than miss the mark of this too often mistaken word.

Identifying what romance means to each of you in the beginning and throughout the getting-to-know-you process and even throughout the relationship, can save frustration and feeling alone while together. The following questions will help you gather answers to introduce and sustain that romantic feeling we all crave.

QUESTIONS TO ASK EACH OTHER

- What does romance mean to you?
- How important is romance to you?
- How important is it to you to have a romantic partner?
- What would you do if your partner wasn't romantic?
- Have you had an unromantic partner in the past? If so, how did you handle it in your relationship?
- Is romance different than sex?
- Describe your perfect romantic morning/evening.
- Do you believe in going on date nights with your partner even after marriage?
- Describe the perfect date night.
- What's one meal you would like to have for a romantic night?
- Is there a specific music genre that gets you going?
- Are public displays of affection (PDAs) romantic to you?
- Are you comfortable showing affection in public? If so, what is your limit?
- Do you like to kiss?
- Do you like to hug?
- What small things brighten up your day when they happen?
- What is one thing you like that makes you feel loved?

- What is the most romantic experience you have ever had?
- What is a romantic fantasy of yours?
- What is your favorite way to be touched?
- What physical action or gesture do you find romantic?
- What is your favorite romance movie?
- What's your favorite romantic comedy?
- What is your favorite love song?
- What do you do on Valentine's Day?
- What is your idea of the perfect romantic gift?
- Are anniversaries important to you?

Notes

_____

_____

_____

_____

_____

_____

_____

_____

_____

_____

3-B: Envisioning Tomorrow

"When you realize you want to spend the rest of your life with somebody, you want the rest of your life to start as soon as possible."
—Harry, When Harry Met Sally

When Syd and I reconnected, I was just about ready to sell my business and move to Curacao to sell coconuts filled with alcohol. That was my dream of retirement. Don't get it twisted, this is still my "retirement goal," but before Syd and I became a couple, we had to discuss our visions of retirement to see if they were compatible. After several conversations over a few months, our joint retirement goal is us selling coconuts filled with tasty libations on a beach in Florida.

Syd didn't have any major issues with my goal/plan, she actually liked the thought. Her only concern was that she didn't want to be more than a four-hour trip away from her mother, children, and future grandchildren so we compromised.

"If you don't know where you're going as a couple, you'll end up somewhere else–like a divorce court."
—Yogi Berra (revised by Les Allen, Jr.)

Sharing your wishes for the future to see if you have common dreams, goals, and expectations is necessary. After all, if you want to be together for the rest of your lives, your desires and goals should be aligned.

If you're a younger couple, take time to consider your future in five or ten-year increments. This will allow you to plan far enough ahead to dream and set goals together for the future. Then you can have annual family planning sessions to review and update your plan.

A fun exercise we recommend to plan your future together is to create a vision board together. This activity will allow both of you to share, discuss, and agree on what you want to accomplish in the future as a team. By creating this board, you will have a visual and tangible reminder of your goals.

Creating a vision board for your life together will allow you to:
- Gain clarity as a couple
- Deepen your connection
- Have accountability
  - Individual goals that pour into family goals
  - Partnership goals that add to the overall family goals
  - Timeframe to achieve the goals

QUESTIONS TO ASK EACH OTHER

- What are your thoughts on having our elderly parents live with us if they can't live on their own one day?
- Have you ever had to take care of an elderly relative/ partner?
- Where would you live if you could live anywhere in the world?
- Would you rather live in a place that has four seasons or

one where it is the same climate all year?

- Where do you think you need to be thinking bigger?
- What is one thing you hope to accomplish in the next five years?
- What would you like your life to be like five (ten/twenty) years from now?
- If you no longer had to work to live comfortably, what would you do with your life?
- How do you envision your lifestyle when you get older?
- If you had to choose a specific age to call yourself old, what age would that be?
- At what age do you plan or expect to retire?
- How do you plan to save for retirement? What are your goals?
- How do you imagine you'll spend your retirement?
- If you were to die today, would you be satisfied with the way you've lived?
- Do you think it is important to plan for tomorrow?
- Do you live for today?
- Are you a long-term planner?
- What is one thing you fear about the future?
- Do you worry about the future?
- How important is it for you and your partner to plan your retirement?
- How important is it for you to live near your children?
- Have you ever created a vision board?

Notes

3-C: In Sickness and In Health

When preparing for a possible future with a potential partner, both physical and mental health needs should be taken into consideration. How does one prepare his or herself to remain healthy both mentally and physically so they can be their best? In sickness and in health is a marital vow that's often undervalued but it can play a significant part in your relationship's overall viability and sustainability.

When I was eight years old, my parents divorced and my father developed kidney disease shortly after. Unsure of this completely, I believe it was my mother's commitment to her marriage that ultimately led to their reconciliation. While this won't be the case for all couples because at times there are irreconcilable differences, one's current and future health has to be considered when you're in a lasting relationship. Unforeseen changes in your partner's health are possible. Going into a long term partnership, there has to be willingness by both parties should health challenges arise. Although there is no way to predict what will occur, having conversations around the ability to be supportive and/or assist despite the illness, are necessary. This includes conversations regarding one another's family's medical and mental health history as many ailments have a genetic predisposition.

If one of you in the relationship encourages a healthy lifestyle including a nutritious diet and regular exercise and the other does not, could this cause a division and create more time apart than together? Absolutely. If one partner chooses to lead a sedentary lifestyle while the other is addicted to outdoors, have you discussed what the compromises will be? Asking and answering questions early is key.

As important as physical health is in a relationship, so is mental health.

Discussing topics such as depression, managing anxiety, anger, and even past traumas is very important as we all have faced or will face emotional challenges. Not understanding how your partner handles these stressors can lead to frustration, resentment, and disconnectedness.

The COVID-19 pandemic has caused a multitude of stressors in marriages by way of the fear of job loss or foreclosure, fear of illness, and overall financial hardship. How do couples handle precautionary measures to protect themselves and their loved ones? If one partner has staunch views regarding vaccinations and the other doesn't, this will complicate household decisions. During times like these, where outside activities can be limiting, being a united team inside can make all the difference in a lasting union.

QUESTIONS TO ASK EACH OTHER

- What is the best decision you've made regarding your health?
- Do you feel healthy? If not, what is your biggest health concern?
- Do you worry about your future health?
- Do you take medication for a health condition? If so, are you compliant with your medication?

- Do you like to exercise? If so, what's your favorite form of exercise?
- Do you work out? How many times a week do you work out?
- How important is it to you that your partner exercise?
- When was the last time you walked for more than an hour?
- Have you ever been on a weight loss program?
- How much sleep do you get each night?
- When was the last time you were sick?
- Do you have any allergies?
- When you are sick, do you require a lot of attention and coddling?
- Are you a good caregiver?
- What are your favorite forms of self-care?
- Are you an emotional eater?
- Are you a smoker?
- Do you mind if your partner smokes?
- Do you drink? If so, how much and how often?
- Do you mind if your partner drinks?
- What are your thoughts on medical marijuana?
- How do you feel about drug use?
- How often do you go to the doctor?
- When do you feel the strongest?
- What have been the most serious injuries or health scares in your life?
- What would you do if you were informed that you have a terminal illness? What would you do if you were informed

that I have a terminal illness?

- How much do you know about your family's health history?
- Did you have any emotional or behavioral issues as a kid?
- Is there a history of mental illness in your family?
- Have you had to live with or spend time with a family member with mental illness?
- What is your view on vaccinations—for adults and for children?
- Have you been vaccinated?

Notes

_____

_____

_____

_____

_____

_____

_____

_____

_____

_____

_____

_____

_____

_____

_____

_____

_____

_____

_____

_____

_____

_____

_____

_____

_____

_____

_____

_____

_____

_____

_____

_____

4-A: When I Think Of Home

Helen Rowland said, home is "any four walls that enclose the right person."

Well, one thing for sure, it takes the right two people and a similar vision of what home means to them to live happily.

When Les and I began talking, I was apprehensive because Les' home was 900 miles, 13 hours and basically a different climate away. Most of my family was in less than a 200-mile radius and so to even consider dating, I had to ask the question who would move and if me, what's it going to be like to leave my home and my people—MOM, children, and besties. I was living in a faster paced metropolitan area, with all four seasons and had been in one house for sixteen years. Contrarily, Les, who had dreamed of one day moving to a warm climate surrounded by water, had found his way to Tampa, Florida and was living in what he described as a tropical oasis in which he had found peace.

As our relationship grew and we made the intentional decision to move forward, this conversation was inevitable. As my children had all graduated from high school and two from college, I had to ponder whether or not it was the right time for me to make such a move. After all, sunny Florida sounded like a great place to be, but was I comfortable with the decision? I would be miles and miles away from my children, mom, and close friends. Not to mention other family challenges so torn was an understatement to say the least. But through faith and prayer, I believed things would ultimately work themselves out.

I was blessed that Les remained patient as I considered all aspects of this life-changing choice and reassured me that if Florida wasn't for me, we could discuss other options. Together we would compromise and determine the best fit for us. It didn't take too long, just about six months before we arrived at the conclusion that we would live similar to "snow birds" chasing the sun!

Deciding where you call home is a mutually agreed upon decision that must be discussed early, honestly, openly, and what else? Intentionally.

Now, when you decide where your castle will be, it's decor, it's energy, and it's flow, your conversation will have to be handled in the same manner because it is a shared space that should be cultivated to both your liking. If there are grave differences in style and/or design within your home, there is bound to be discomfort experienced by one or both of you.

Throughout the different cycles of life, there may be a need to make decisions around moving. It may be related to work, child(ren), aging parents, or the like. It is important to remember these early discussions and compromises as they become part of your relationship's foundation.

QUESTIONS TO ASK EACH OTHER

- What is your definition of home?
- What is the first thing you think of when you hear the word home?

- Where do you consider home to be?
- Is it important to own your home?
- Have you ever purchased a home on your own?
- Have you ever moved to a new state on your own?
- How many different states/cities have you lived in?
- Would you be flexible about relocating to another city or state?
- Is there any place you would not move to?
- Is there a particular climate you would prefer your home be in?
- What is the farthest you would move from your parents, kids, and siblings?
- Are you comfortable with your (or your partner's) adult children living in your home?
- Are you comfortable with your (or your partner's) aging parents living in your home?
- Are you comfortable working from home?
- Are you comfortable being at home alone?
- Are there any conditions that would be unacceptable in your home?
- Do you enjoy hosting visitors in your home?
- Do you require people to take off their shoes when they enter your home?
- Do you have any rules that people have to adhere to when they visit?
- Do you allow pets in your home?

Notes

4-B: More Than Four Walls

Cold or Hot? Pitch black versus night light? Silence or background noise? Courting is one thing, living together full-time is another. The intentionality in the courtship phase must continue as you are now predetermining household compatibility. What are those differences that could create tension and how can you manage on a daily basis?

Couples are certainly more successful when they can work together as a team. When one lives alone, it's easy to procrastinate on what needs to be done. In essence, to become complacent. But it's another ballgame when your actions or inactions at home impact your partner. You don't want minor things to snowball into bigger challenges and become sources of frustration and resentment. Through healthy conversation and mutual respect, compatibility at home can be achieved. Don't assume, expect, demand, question, or judge before this talk.

Two committed people in a partnership have several shared responsibilities. One significant responsibility is running the household which includes managing the bills, cleaning, cooking, yard work, and figuring out child care among other things. In our Intentional Courting Model, we encourage all couples to set their priorities as a couple. If you are both neat freaks, or both slobs, chances are you would be problem free. But if one isn't comfortable with a messy home, and the other is, compromise is necessary.

My husband and I determined that our time should be equal since we have the same number of minutes in a day. This works for us as there are no assumed roles or rules based on gender. We discussed early how we both valued our time and committed to creating an agreed upon household schedule.

We recommend you discuss the chores you are comfortable with as well as those you absolutely detest. Have your partner do the same. Flush through this list first and determine a time table, taking into consideration that someone may be a morning person while the other is a night owl. Remember, with many things we do in life, timing is key.

Meet frequently to assess whether or not the plan established is working. If it's not, try to figure out the areas in which there is reluctance. Perhaps someone overcommitted too soon or even underestimated the time required for a certain chore.

Talk through likes, dislikes, preferences and flat out non-negotiables around household expectations and habits. Ensure there is mutual agreement and check in periodically to make sure the plan still works. It only works, if you work at it!

QUESTIONS TO ASK EACH OTHER

- How important is a clean house to you?
- How should housework be divided?
- What is your least favorite household chore?
- What is your favorite household chore?
- How often do you think the house should be cleaned?
- How often do you clean your toilets?
- What is the best way to communicate with you about chores?

- How do you feel about outsourcing certain responsibilities like cleaning?
- Do you expect each of us to do our own laundry?
- Do you believe in cleaning out the microwave?
- What are some of the challenges you've had in past relationships related to household responsibility?
- How would you rate your level of cleanliness?
- Do you make up your bed daily?
- Do you believe pets should be allowed in the kitchen?
- What rules or practices did your household follow growing up that you would also implement in your own home? What rules or practices would you choose not to follow?
- Should children help with household chores?
- Are you a morning person or a night owl?
- When do you feel most productive with household chores?
- On what temperature do you like to keep the interior of the house?
- What are your thoughts on wearing shoes in the house?
- When you sleep, do you like it to be cold or warm?
- When you sleep, do you use a fan or other noise device?
- When you sleep, do you like the room to be pitch black?
- Do you sleep with the door open or closed?
- Do you sleep with the windows open or closed?
- What do you do with a dish immediately after using it?
- Do you fold your laundry right away or wait a few days?

Notes

4-C: Life is What You Bake It!

No matter how you look at it, food and cooking are a big part of our relationships.

One recent study noted that eighty-seven percent of couples surveyed believe cooking is one of the top activities couples can do to strengthen their relationship. Cooking is an expression of love. Cooking allows couples to connect, to be creative together, and research shows that while cooking, couples can experience the same feelings they experience while giving love or being loved. And, when one cooks for their partner, it's a love language on its own. Imagine one partner who does not love to cook but has a hot meal waiting when their significant other arrives home. Imagine how much more that gesture is appreciated. As much as cooking alone or together has its positives, it is still an area that requires attention.

Determining likes and dislikes around cooking is critical in a partnership. What if your partner hates to cook and your expectation is that they do? There are several suggestions for this but you wouldn't know how to navigate if you don't plan around it. The Intentional Courting Model (ICM) supports healthy discussions around food preferences and habits.

What is the expectation around meal preparation? In my household, I do not like to cook and neither does my husband. We discussed this early on. While he mentioned that it was great in previous relationships to have a hot meal on the table, he was also ok with being involved in it or planning so it still happens. Ask about preferences and do not assume it's someone's job or contrarily, a shared task, unless that has been decided.

Discuss how you can compromise and come up with a plan that works. Maybe each of you cooks two nights per week and the other three nights, you order take out. Maybe you will cook together during the week and indulge in restaurant hopping over the weekend. Maybe one weekend a month you will cook numerous meals that can be frozen and later taken out to feed the family for a week. It doesn't matter how it's done, it matters that there is agreement on how it's done. That's the intentional way, intending to make a decision to agree, rather than disagreeing without prior intent.

In addition to cooking itself, what have you decided about meal times? About the clean up? When one cooks, does the other clean? Is eating together as a family important, unimportant, or just important to one of you? Agree to set ground rules for the kitchen in the early phases of this partnership.

And remember, there is so much emphasis on conscious eating. Many people have become vegan and gone to plant-based diets. As there are an abundance of grocery stores, restaurants, and recipes to support them, it doesn't replace the understanding and support from one's partner. Respecting each other's decision and compromising when you can is vital. Finding restaurants you both will enjoy and cooking meals that satisfy both palettes will make it work for your union, not to mention invite a little spice to your life.

QUESTIONS TO ASK EACH OTHER

- Can you cook?
- Do you like to cook?
- What is your least favorite food to cook?
- What is your favorite meal?
- Do you like gourmet meals?
- Are you ok with simple meals or do you prefer non-traditional meals?
- Would you ever eat breakfast for dinner?
- Is a sandwich adequate or are you always looking for a three course meal?
- How would you feel if your partner didn't cook?
- Do you prefer to cook or eat out?
- What's your favorite kitchen smell?
- Do you tend to over season or under season your food?
- If I cook, will you clean?
- Do you think someone cooking for you is romantic?
- Do you believe cooking together as a couple can strengthen our relationship?
- Would you be ok with the idea of a catered Thanksgiving dinner?
- Do you like to cook for large gatherings?

Notes

_____

_____

_____

_____

_____

_____

_____

_____

_____

_____

_____

_____

_____

_____

_____

_____

_____

_____

_____

_____

4-D: Furry Family Members

One of my best friends had to let her significant other know that she and her pup were a package deal. Although things didn't go as planned after that, it turns out it was for the best because she absolutely adored animals and he suffered from cynophobia (the fear of dogs), along with roughly eight percent of the population. Even with pets, it is crucial to review your non-negotiables early so you are choosing the best option for you.

Pets can be problematic in a relationship when two persons are on opposite sides of the fence with a furry friend. "American pet owners are transforming the cultural definition of family; dogs and cats are treated like children, siblings, and grandchildren."

When you are intentionally dating/courting someone with a pet, understand the nature of the relationship. Dogs are often viewed as part of the family to some, and simply as an animal to someone else. As a family member, there are a number of feelings attached, which produces a great deal of responsibility and loyalty.

When Les and I began dating, in addition to being a mother to three children, I was a mother to a four pound Yorkie named Harley. Some of my earlier trips to Florida included Harley, and one time she had to be left in Les' care while I traveled out of the country. Les had not owned a pet for more than a decade and the responsibilities of pet ownership weighed heavy on him. But he made a decision to accept Harley as part of the package and knew she had to be taken care of in my absence.

Can you handle this on a long-term basis? Can you handle

having to share time, perhaps even tasks, around your partner's animal? Are you able to be tolerant of certain challenges that come with pet ownership, such as making arrangements for pets when traveling, medical expenses, time taken for training, and potential household accidents?

In our ICM, we would like you to flush out these areas early in the getting-to-know-you phase to determine whether or not the two of you and your friendly or not-so-friendly feline can coexist.

QUESTIONS TO ASK EACH OTHER

- Are you comfortable with animals around you?
- Did you grow up with pets in your home?
- What pets have you had?
- Do you currently have a pet? If so, what kind?
- What is its name? How did you choose this name?
- What is your pet peeve with regards to owning a pet?
- How would you feel if your partner had several animals?
- Are you afraid of any animals?
- Who takes care of it when you are not at home?
- Do you have to bring your pet wherever you go?
- Do you travel with your pet?
- How much and how often does the pet eat?
- How much and how often does the pet go outside?
- How much and how often does the pet defecate?
- Do you believe in getting vaccinations for your pet?

- Would you pay for an obedience class for a dog?
- If you own a dog, what breed do you prefer?
- How do you deal with bad pet behaviors?
- Do you have an issue cleaning up a pet's urine/poop?
- If you don't have a pet, why not?

Notes

_____

_____

_____

_____

_____

_____

_____

_____

_____

_____

_____

_____

_____

_____

4-E: Hang All The Mistletoe

Amazon deliveries from Thanksgiving up to Christmas Eve? Not one, not two, not three, but four Christmas trees decorated throughout the house? BOSE speakers blasting Christmas songs while the family is dressed up in this year's themed Christmas pajamas?

Or maybe a candy cane here and there, but more so a day off from work, family, fun and some football? Which category are you in or is there a degree of overlap between the two?

In the States, there are twelve permanent federal holidays. They range from holidays that are most commonly celebrated, those observed with paid time off, those with religious significance, and those with cultural or historical significance. It is very helpful in a new relationship that has potential for a long-term future to discuss your actual preferences around the holidays.

For many, holidays can be a source of pain and longing. Often, memories of loved ones who have transitioned, and reminiscing childhood traditions or other memories, can create intense feelings, both joyful and sad.

There are several triggers that increase depression during this time. It could be the first holiday season after the passing of a family member. These feelings of grief and loss can be challenging to manage. Someone prone to the Holiday Blues who has hopes of the holiday passing by quickly can directly conflict with one who relishes in this festive time. Holidays can also be a time of great financial stress. Balancing bills and gifts for the family can be difficult.

Holidays bring together family and loved ones, and some down time, and it's important to not only understand your partner's expectations, but their desires, fears, and challenges around the day as well.

What is the key to success? Here's a hint. It's the answer in almost every chapter. Communication. More specifically, communicating early and often. There's nothing more merry and bright than a good understanding and ultimate acceptance of your partner.

QUESTIONS TO ASK EACH OTHER

- How important are birthdays, anniversaries, and other holidays?
- What was your most memorable holiday as a child?
- What are your favorite holiday treats?
- What is your funniest holiday memory?
- What's your favorite holiday?
- What is your favorite holiday scent?
- How did you spend your holidays last year?
- How will you spend the holidays next year?
- Is gift giving important to you during the holidays? Are some holidays more important than others? If so, which and why? (Christmas, Valentine's Day, Mother's Day, Father's Day, Sweetest Day)
- How would you feel if your partner spent an excessive amount on holiday gifts?

- How would you feel if your partner was "tight" about spending and didn't believe in lavish gifts?
- Do you expect to get an expensive gift for Christmas?
- What is a new tradition you want to make happen this year?
- In what ways would you like to give to others during the holidays?
- What would be the best holiday date?
- What are your favorite winter activities?
- How do you envision splitting holidays between your family and your significant other's?
- Would it be ok to be apart during the holidays?
- Is it important to be with your adult children during the holidays?
- What's your dream family holiday destination?
- What's your dream couple holiday destination?
- Do you like to decorate your home for any holidays or all holidays?
- Would it be ok to not decorate your home?

Notes

_____

_____

_____

_____

_____

4-F: Planned Escapes

Are you a true vacationer? Or is your vacation executed down to each detail encompassing a week of planned activities without downtime? Funny, I guess I just described my not-so-ideal vacation. But remember, that's subjective as planning to some could be ideal. I like to know what's on the agenda but not necessarily be bound to it. Nonetheless, that's the intent of this chapter and book ultimately. To determine compatibility in several key areas, including travel.

Fortunately, Les and I quickly discovered that we both were really good at relaxing. In the hustle and bustle of our daily lives, we have meetings, phone calls, meetings, counseling sessions, meetings, contracts to review and did I mention meetings? So on vacation, we truly want to vacation. We realized creating a very casual go-with-the-flow itinerary worked best for us and was just what we needed to make for an enjoyable getaway.

But what if two people's idea of vacationing was polar opposite? During courtship, Les shared that in one of his previous relationships, his partner planned every minute of the vacation and for him, that was extremely stressful. Planning, money, energy, and lots of time go into creating each vacation so if your compatibility while there is not aligned, there will be some bumps on the trip. Vacations together then become something that a couple won't necessarily look forward to. They can become times when there's unnecessary angst and maybe even turn into a future pledge to girls trips and fellas only excursions.

Talk through your idea of a perfect vacation from location of destination, to a desirable resort, restaurant choices, activities, amount of money you'll spend, and how much you won't spend bringing back those annoying souvenirs for family members you never see.

Talking through and compromising can help make a couple's experiences while away fun and stress free and create an anticipation of future travels.

QUESTIONS TO ASK EACH OTHER

- Where have you traveled?
- Describe your perfect vacation?
- Ideally, how many vacations would you like to take per year?
- How long is your ideal vacation?
- Would you be ok if your partner wanted to or preferred to travel alone?
- How would you feel about a significant other going on a girls trip or a fellas trip?
- What was your favorite place to go when you were a child?
- What's the best road trip you've been on?
- Do you like long road trips?
- What is the longest time you want be in a car for a road trip?
- How many countries outside of the US have you visited?
- If you could travel to any country in the world for one month, where would you go?

- How do you feel about international travel?
- Where is the last place you'd ever go?
- If you could make a travel bucket list, what are your top three cities?
- What stresses you out the most when traveling?
- How do you feel about group vacations with other couples?
- What is your ideal couples vacation?
- Do you tend to under pack or overpack?
- Are you open to any/every mode of transportation to get to your destination?
- How do you feel about flying?
- What travel role would you like to play? (i.e., trip organizer, activities specialist, or driver.)

Notes

_____

_____

_____

_____

_____

_____

_____

4-G: Becoming One

Do you dream of having a huge wedding, with a reception that feels like an awards show? What if your future partner is seeking a private destination wedding somewhere on the beach. What would you do? How would you handle this difference in desires?

I have witnessed too many couples that have had spectacular wedding events, end up paying on the wedding debt long after they've divorced. Sometimes the expense in planning the wedding ceremony created a stress point in the relationship that moved from a crack to a canyon. Discuss each other's dream wedding ideas so you will have time to plan a ceremony that reflects the desires of each of you. By doing this, you won't mind the work and expense that go into creating your dream ceremony. Learning how to work together as a team, compromising and working side by side, will help you accomplish this important goal.

While Syd and I were planning our wedding, there were several things going on that made planning the wedding ceremony a huge task. We were united on the location, the guest list, and our date. Instead, our stress was from managing the responsibilities of our careers. Here are a few of the issues we were trying to work around in order to have the ceremony we wanted.

- Everything that goes into planning a destination wedding in the Caribbean
- Managing/handling a merger at Sydney's office
- Preparing a house for new tenants
- Adult kids (Chicago, Maryland, D.C., Los Angeles & Dallas – with varying schedules and responsibilities) and

figuring out itinerary to and from the wedding on their tight schedules

- Running BlackStar, Les' personal business
- ...and oh yeah, a global pandemic

Syd's stress was not only visible, but palpable. We decided we didn't want to delay the wedding date but things were becoming overwhelming. Since we had decided on the date and the type of location, we made the decision to scrap our smaller destination wedding for an even smaller intimate wedding ceremony with no guests other than the pastor. On the day of the wedding, Sydney's parents—who I surprised her with and my line brother who lives in our destination location, were in attendance. He was instrumental in helping me plan, and he and his wife were witnesses to our special day.

Having those parameters, I knew that I could take on planning the wedding which would allow Sydney time to focus on her job and managing the sensitive and delicate task of combing through sixteen years of family items and heirlooms so we could leave the house on time. I asked her if she trusted me, she said she did. I told her I would handle the wedding and it would be a surprise location and she agreed. We had a beautiful destination wedding on November 11, 2021 at 11 AM in Miami, Florida. I say all this to say, when two people intentionally choose to make a decision and trust one another in its execution, many things can be accomplished.

We were able to have the wedding ceremony that we both wanted because we compromised. She trusted me because we went through the process that we are sharing with you in this guide, our Intentional Courtship Model. The more you are open and honest with each other and ask tough questions, the more trust you build with each other. Period.

QUESTIONS TO ASK EACH OTHER

- What do you believe is most important in a marriage (i.e., communication, trust, etc.)?
- Have you been married before?
- How many times have you been married?
- What do you consider the pros and cons of marriage?
- What if your partner did not want to get married but was okay with staying together long term?
- Would you marry someone who has not been married before?
- Would you date someone who has been married multiple times?
- What are your thoughts on divorce?
- What type of wedding ceremony do you want?
- Do you want your wedding ceremony to be religious, non-religious, or something in the middle?
- Would you ever consider eloping?
- Where would you like to have your wedding ceremony?
- How big of a wedding ceremony do you want?
- What is your ideal wedding ceremony budget?
- Would you hire a wedding planner?

- How soon would you want to get married after dating?
- Would you keep your maiden name, use a hyphenated last name, or take on your spouse's last name?
- Do you believe marriage is necessary before having a child together?
- Would you get married because you became pregnant?
- If you discover something you don't like after tying the knot, what would you do?
- What are the top two things that would end your marriage?

Notes

_____

_____

_____

_____

_____

_____

_____

_____

_____

_____

_____

_____

4-H: Saving The Best For Last

After I divorced, as a single mom, I was ready to play! But playing came with high costs—particularly my feelings. I jumped in a few situations and pretended that no matter what, I wouldn't catch feelings. But guess what? I did exactly that. Not only was I fooling myself, I was allowing myself to be used which was the worst feeling.

Although I have since thrown away these experiences, I have kept the valuable lessons learned from them. I learned that even the nicest of people will treat you the way you allow them to. This is why you have to set boundaries and realize that without them, you invite disrespect into your life.

My hope is to spare someone out there, especially my dear daughters, by helping them understand that sex doesn't equal love. For some, it doesn't even equal like. To many, simply put, it is just pleasurable exercise. Situationships get old and so does meaningless sex.

If your goal is to be intentional, but it isn't theirs, STOP. If they make it clear that they don't want a relationship and they still want sex, STOP. Do not think you can change their mind. Your looks, intelligence, or your W.A.P. will not make a difference. When they clearly speak it and/or let their actions show it, you must clearly hear them. Be intentional, move on, love yourself more, and keep preparing for the partner that is ready for you.

Let's Talk About Sex…

Sex, in many families, is something we learn to avoid talking about. However, as we mature and understand the importance of our sexual health, we understand the importance of exploring it to determine compatibility.

When exploring intentional courting, timing is everything and sex can be one of those subjects you don't want to talk about too soon. In your journey with your potential partner, decide when the time is right. Be deliberate about asking and learning about each other's sex practices, current and past history of STDs, and sexual boundaries. Is there anything on your non-negotiable list when it comes to sex? What are your thoughts on waiting? Explore these before committing, and don't be afraid to stand by your beliefs.

Although learning of your partner's sexual past may not be easy, it can be discussed, with sensitivity and understanding. As this can be a touchy subject, there should be respect, without judgment. Everyone has a past. For some, being able to expose "dirty secrets" takes a great deal of self-love and growth. Others, maybe less. Nonetheless, talking about your past sexual history can have its share of benefits. Open and honest conversation can foster closeness and connection. And eventually, from these conversations, deeper intimacy may develop.

Understand the purpose of why you are sharing. For you both, is it important to share sexual histories? Is it for general knowledge? Does it have an impact on what is happening in the present? Or do you feel like it is something that should be disclosed because it may come up? Once you know the purpose, you will better know the right time to bring it up.

Being okay with our sexual pasts is the goal. As humans, we make mistakes from which we (hopefully) learn and grow. Our past does not define us.

Don't make the mistake of falling into a comparison trap feeling like you won't measure up to someone from your partner's past. We are all different and often, we create a more colorful and interesting story in our head. Feelings of inadequacy can go both ways. That's why open, honest, and transparent communication helps. In my experience, it's a lot easier to discuss sex and ask and answer the tough questions before you get in bed together. Once you start sleeping together, the intent of some questions may be misunderstood. Not to say you shouldn't talk about sex once you've started having it, but frequent and ongoing questions about one's sexual history can send the wrong message.

Sexual compatibility in a relationship is underestimated. Humans are sexual creatures and sex is essential to physical and emotional happiness. When couples are not able to fulfill each other's sexual desires, trouble cometh with all of its associates.

We don't often prioritize sexual compatibility because it is an uncomfortable topic. Unfortunately, there is still a degree of shame and awkwardness when talking about sex. When couples date, if there is unhappiness in the bedroom, the blame is often shifted to money or communication when sex may very well be the culprit. Research supports this and that same research confirms that sex is a major cause of marital discord.

In your intentional journey, talk to your partner early about sex. Be open about your needs, desires, kinks, and fetishes. This is especially important once you are married or headed down that road. Sometimes our partners don't know what we desire until it's too late.

Going through the questions in this chapter, when the time is right, will lead you down the right path. Maybe you will share it all upfront or maybe you will share more details down the road. Either way works.

I wish I had been more intentional in some of my choices after divorce. Too many times I ignored the obvious. I learned for sure but I hope this book inspires others to avoid my mistakes, especially our daughters. I hope their journeys are more deliberate for their minds, bodies, and souls.

QUESTIONS TO ASK EACH OTHER

- How important do you think sex is in our relationship?
- How well do you think our sex drives match up?
- What if your partner's sex drive was a lot different from yours?
- Do you believe it's necessary to discuss sexually transmitted diseases?
- What if your partner discloses that they have an STD, what would you do?
- Besides orgasms, what is the best part of sex?
- What do you never get tired of?
- In terms of intimacy, what's getting worse and worse as you get older?
- What's getting better and better as you get older?
- How do you communicate when you're in the mood?

- What do you like your partner to do in bed that turns you on?
- Is it important to know about your partner's former lovers?
- What's your favorite place to have sex?
- What's your favorite type of foreplay?
- Would you rather have more frequent sex or better sex?
- Would you be open to using props in bed?
- How many times do you masturbate a week?
- Do you talk about your sex life with friends and family?
- What do you fantasize about?
- Ideally how many times a week would you want to have sex?
- What part of the body turns you on the most?
- Do you like being surprised when you have sex?
- What kind of talk do you like, if any, in bed?
- What time of day do you most prefer to have sex?
- What three things make someone good in bed?
- Do you have any unfulfilled sexual desires or fantasies?
- How would you respond to a third person joining?
- Is there anything you won't do in bed?
- Apart from sex what other activity makes you feel close?
- Is there a sex position you want to try but haven't?
- What does it mean to be good in bed?
- What's better than great sex?
- Describe the physical touch that best communicates "I love you."

Notes

Part 9
Our Intentional Love
Loving Intentionally

FLYING WITHOUT BAGS

As of today, Syd and I are flying without bags. Meaning, since we've reconnected, we are feeling freer, lighter, and without excess baggage. You see, when you travel without bags, it's akin to being a wealthy traveler. The kind that walks through the airport with a small Gucci, Louie, or Coach leather duffle bag. They don't go and drop-off bags when they check in. They walk directly from their vehicle to their gate with one bag.

I used to wonder, *how does someone travel like that?* I always seemed to overpack and had to take my luggage to the car, unload it in the parking garage, and then drag it to the airport ticket counter. Then once I landed at my destination, I had to wait for my luggage to arrive on the carousel, drag it to the rental car shuttle, to the rental car, to the front desk at the hotel, and finally into the hotel room. Now I'm tired. Then guess what, after a few days, I'd have to do it all over again to get home. It was an exhausting experience.

In the ICM, you unpack early and efficiently so baggage is left behind. You don't keep it, store it, or put it in your closet only to pull it out again. You don't give it to your spouse, your children, or newcomers. You learn and let it go. You are finally free.

Now, in the realm of relationships, I travel in life and love like a wealthy traveler. I'm what they call a "day bagger." I intentionally travel with only who and what I need. I am traveling in a powerful, light, and liberated way.

When you've taken the requisite time to work on yourself, learn who you are, what you are, where you want to go, what you're willing to accept, what's a deal breaker, and then love who you are—you'll know you don't need to carry all that extra luggage any longer. The great thing is that Syd and I were in the same space when we reconnected. We had finally discovered ourselves and we were ready for takeoff.

Just imagine when you and your potential partner/spouse are traveling without luggage. Regardless of your method of traveling, you will get to your destination faster, and more efficiently since you are carrying less weight. However you are traveling, you will move with greater ease as your burden is lighter.

Also, consider when you and your partner are starting at the same point (alignment), you will have minimal distractions because you (the team) know where you want to go. There is less wasted energy and time because you are jointly on a mission to get to your destination.

Now that we are at the end of this guidebook, we hope you know what we mean when we say "loving intentionally." As a reminder, it means being in or developing a love that brings you daily fulfillment and grows into a lifelong mutually beneficial love/partnership/relationship. You don't get there by haphazardly dating anyone. You get there by pushing your desire to have a great partner/spouse (good intentions) into having a great partner/spouse (loving intentionally). Be intentional: choose the person that will continually, habitually, and proactively fulfill you. Get out of the game, stop looking, and start prepping today!

Our Thanks

We hope you noticed these recurring words and themes throughout *Intentional 4Play*. Each is important to intentional dating, intentional courting, and intentional living.

Intentional
Non-Negotiable
STOP
Ask Hard Questions
Listen
Respect
Alignment
Being Open & Honest
Compromise
Research
Trust
Value Time

Congratulations on getting to this point in the book! While you've picked up some new tools and resources, the work is just beginning. Try to avoid putting this book on your bookshelf and leaving it there even when you are in a successful long-term relationship. Pull it off of the shelf occasionally to realign your relationship.

Remember in an intentional journey, there is no guessing. You don't have to wonder IF, because you already know WHEN. It has been talked about and agreed upon. Stop settling for IF!

Don't let your heart outpace your head. Ask clarifying questions without being afraid to do so. Then move based on those answers coupled with their actions. That's the Intentional Courting Model way. PERIODT.

We hope you have enjoyed learning more about our journey and feel better prepared for your own. We pray that you too will find an intentional partner. Remember, stop looking and start preparing. The rest will fall into place.

Thank you again for your support.

Peace & Blessings.

Special Acknowledgments

I have so many people to thank for planting seeds of inspiration within me. Beyond my ancestors, I will not list any names here, as I would be remiss if I mistakenly leave someone out. Please know that I have received your seeds of inspiration, the libations of knowledge you have poured into me, and the anointing of wisdom that has nourished me. These items support the strong vine I am becoming. Also, know that I humbly accept the pruning that growth requires.

A Special Thank You to:
My Planters: Leslie Allen, Sr., Shirley Allen, Velvie Norman, Velvie Green, Ruth Allen, Ruben Allen, and Kenneth Young
My Trellises: Herm, Erik, and Tego
My Fruit: Ayanna Simone & Amani Leslie
My Bonus Fruit: Geno, KJ, Lexi, Brie, Ciara, and Justin
My Water/Love: Sydney, my wife, thank you for loving me with intention.

—Les Allen, Jr.

Giving thanks to:
God, who made all this possible!
My mom, whose steadfast example of love and strength molded me into the woman I am today.
My daughters, Brielle Nicole, and Ciara Autumn, whose existence has made me set the bar higher and given me so much joy, purpose, and reasons to be intentional.

My son, Justin Isaiah, who has made me a better human being and taught me the true depth of unconditional LOVE.

My precious grandbaby, Blaise, who I watched BOLDLY make her entrance into the world, as long as I have breath, you will KNOW how much I love you.

My godmommy, Wanda, who will always be a bright constant in my life and my children's lives. And Kya, who is a constant in my life and my children's lives.

My "Ride or Dies," Kya, Raegen, Cassandra, Nicola, LaTarsha, Pam, Kurtae, Alethia, Dreana, and Nicole

My aunties, Alicia, Sylvia, Barbara, Gwen, Linda

And to my village, Herb, my Dear Lex, and my whole Brown family, thanks for your never-ending LOVE.

And to Les—my Les—the best intentional decision I have made. Baby, thanks for being my husband & friend. We did it!

As Unc says, GOOD!

—*Sydney Allen*